At Issue

| Genetically
| Engineered Food

Other Books in the At Issue Series:

At Issue

Genetically Engineered Food

Debra A. Miller, Book Editor

GREENHAVEN PRESS
A part of Gale, Cengage Learning

GALE
CENGAGE Learning·

Detroit • New York • San Francisco • New Haven, Conn • Waterville, Maine • London

Elizabeth Des Chenes, *Director, Publishing Solutions*

© 2012 Greenhaven Press, a part of Gale, Cengage Learning

Gale and Greenhaven Press are registered trademarks used herein under license.

For more information, contact:
Greenhaven Press
27500 Drake Rd.
Farmington Hills, MI 48331-3535
Or you can visit our Internet site at gale.cengage.com

For product information and technology assistance, contact us at

Gale Customer Support, 1-800-877-4253
For permission to use material from this text or product, submit all requests online at
www.cengage.com/permissions

Further permissions questions can be emailed to permissionrequest@cengage.com

Articles in Greenhaven Press anthologies are often edited for length to meet page require-ments. In addition, original titles of these works are changed to clearly present the main thesis and to explicitly indicate the author's opinion. Every effort is made to ensure that Greenhaven Press accurately reflects the original intent of the authors. Every effort has been made to trace the owners of copyrighted material.

Cover image © Images.com/Corbis.

LIBRARY OF CONGRESS CATALOGING-IN-PUBLICATION DATA

Genetically engineered food / Debra A. Miller, book editor.
    p. cm. -- (At issue)
    Includes bibliographical references and index.
    ISBN 978-0-7377-5572-5 (hardcover) -- ISBN 978-0-7377-5573-2 (pbk.)
    1. Genetically modified foods. 2. Genetically modified foods--Moral and ethical aspects. 3. Genetically modified foods--Government policy. 4. Food--Biotechnology. I. Miller, Debra A.
    TP248.65.F66G45 2011
    641.3--dc23

                                                                    2011048274

Printed in the United States of America
1 2 3 4 5 6 7 16 15 14 13 12

Contents

Introduction

Genetically engineered (GE) food, also called genetically modified (GM) food, is the product of a new biotech industry that has only existed since the late 20th century, but which has grown phenomenally during that period. The first GE food was marketed in 1994, and in 2010, according to industry expert the International Service for the Acquisition of Agri-biotech Applications (ISAAA), the world's farmers planted almost 366 million acres (148 million hectares) of genetically modified crops in 29 different countries. Clive James, author of a recent ISAAA report, explains, "Growth remains strong, with biotech hectarage increasing 14 million hectares (34.6 million acres)—or 10 percent—between 2009 and 2010."[1] The United States leads the world in GE crops and many developing countries have also embraced this technology, but many European countries have imposed strict barriers on the planting of GE crops and sale of GE foods. Yet even in America, GE foods and crops remain controversial because many consumers and consumer groups worry about their impact on human health, the environment, and the global agriculture industry.

GE foods are basically foods derived from plant seeds that have had their DNA changed using genetic engineering techniques. Farmers have been changing plant DNA for decades using a slower, more natural, but less predictable process of selectively breeding plant species with other plant species to breed out unwanted traits or breed in desired traits. Genetic engineering, however, accomplishes DNA changes very quickly by directly adding to or subtracting from the DNA in plants. The most typical type of genetic modifications have been made to produce fruit and vegetable species that are resistant

1. Clive James, "Rapid Rate of Global Growth for Biotech Crops," US Grains Council, Southeast Farm Press via Western Farm Press, August 24, 2011.

to herbicides and pesticides. This has allowed farmers to spray chemicals on crops to kill weeds and pests without concern that those chemicals will kill or damage the crops themselves. The biotechnology company that is the world's leading producer of GE seeds is the Missouri-based Monsanto company. Monsanto has developed several types of seeds—such as soybeans, corn, cotton, and wheat—that are resistant to its herbicide glyphosate, which it markets as Roundup.

The GE story began in the early 1990s when the California company Calegne (later acquired by Monsanto) developed a type of GE tomato, called Flavor Savr. Approved for human consumption in 1992, Flavor Savr tomatoes were genetically modified to ripen without softening, making it easier for the fruit to be picked and shipped to consumer markets without damage. Most GE crops are still grown in North America, and it is very difficult for consumers to avoid GE foods, because they are in a wide variety of crops—such as soybeans, corn, cotton, papaya, tomatoes, canola, sugar cane and rice—and because GE foods are not labeled.

On the other hand, a number of countries have banned the use of some or all types of GE seed. Venezuela, for example, instituted a broad ban, along with several countries in Europe, including France, Germany, Austria, Hungary, Bulgaria, Luxembourg, and Greece—all of which completely ban GE corn. And many Europeans would like to see a Europe-wide ban on GE crops that would prevent the planting of GE seeds anywhere within the European Union (EU), an economic and political union that covers 27 countries.

The concerns about GE crops revolve around potential impacts on human health and the environment. Critics claim that GE crops have not been studied enough by independent researchers and may be linked to recent increases in allergic reactions and a host of other health problems. In addition, organic farmers and others fear that GE crops could spread uncontrollably in the environment, contaminating organic crops and animals and affecting the natural environment in as yet unknown ways. Already there is some evidence that the use of Roundup-resistant seeds and crops have led to new types of superweeds, causing farmers to spray more toxic herbicide chemicals on food crops in an effort to contain the new weed species. GE critics worry that nature will always find a way to trump human GE inventions, leading to even more toxic food if weeds and pests cannot be easily controlled, and possibly to widespread damage to the agricultural industry itself. Other potential problems with GE technology involve the fact that it allows the transfer of genes from animals to plants and vice-versa; this does not occur in nature and it raises the specter of yet unknown ramifications. GE food producers have already inserted an insect-resistance gene from the natural pesticide bacterium Bacillus thuringiensis (Bt) into corn plants, producing Bt corn, but many scientists predict that this will lead to the growth of Bt-resistant pests, eliminating the effectiveness of a natural pesticide that organic farmers have used for decades. GE critics would like to see much more stringent regulation and testing of GE products, and at the very least, they want GE foods to be labeled so that consumers can avoid them if they wish.

GE proponents, however, largely dismiss these concerns, noting that almost 20 years of experience has led to very little in the way of proven health or environmental damage. The world, supporters say, needs GE products because they can increase crop yields at a time of increasing populations and rising food prices. GE food producers also claim that by allowing better control of weeds and pests, GE crops actually help to reduce the use of harmful herbicides and pesticides; increase crop yields; and allow for no-till (no plowing) farming that improves soil quality, uses less fossil fuel energy, and reduces carbon emissions that contribute to global warming. There is no need to label GE foods, supporters say, because they are no different from non-GE foods in terms of their levels of nutrition or other characteristics. Labeling, they warn, would stigmatize GE foods and ruin the biotechnology industry. GE boosters see a future in which biotechnology could help improve nutrition and health in developing countries. By developing GE crops that are resistant to drought and salt, more crops could be grown in arid or saline-contaminated soils, increasing global food production, and GE crops that contain vitamins or vaccines for diseases could greatly aid in the fight against hunger and disease. GE critics question many of these claimed current and future benefits, noting that most GE products so far have been developed in order to produce profits for biotech companies, rather than for environmental or humanitarian purposes.

Despite the continuing controversy surrounding GE foods, US regulatory agencies have continued to expand the number of GE products on the American market. In 2011, the US Department of Agriculture approved three new kinds of GE crops—alfalfa (which is widely used to feed cattle), a type of corn (grown to produce ethanol), and sugar beets. Most experts also expect the US Food and Drug Administration to approve the production and sale of a fast-growing GE salmon. Critics warn that the approval of alfalfa and ethanol corn will almost certainly lead to GE contamination of both organic foods and the entire food supply, since it will be impossible to keep them from infecting non-GE crops fed to food animals. And critics worry that the GE salmon could pollute wild salmon populations as well. The authors of the viewpoints included in *At Issue: Genetically Engineered Food* help to illuminate many of the issues in this debate about GE foods.

1

Genetically Engineered Foods Are Hazardous

Ronnie Cummins

Ronnie Cummins is the founder of the Organic Consumers Association (OCA), a non-profit organization that promotes organic foods and sustainable agriculture.

Genetic engineering (GE) allows global biotechnology companies to create and legally own new forms of plants and animals. These new GE products are unpredictable and could be a threat to humans, animals, and the environment. GE foods, for example, have been found to contain toxins, some of them deadly and others cancer-causing. In addition, GE foods could harm people with allergies by exposing them to proteins spliced into common food products. And GE crops can offer less nutrition, lead to antibiotic resistance, and often contain as many or even more toxic pesticides than non-GE crops. GE crops also pose a threat to traditional and organic methods of farming. GE technology must be banned.

The technology of Genetic Engineering (GE) is the practice of altering or disrupting the genetic blueprints of living organisms—plants, trees, fish, animals, humans, and microorganisms. This technology is wielded by transnational "life science" corporations such as Monsanto and Aventis, who patent these blueprints, and sell the resulting gene-foods, seeds, or other products for profit. Life science corporations proclaim that their new products will make agriculture sustainable, eliminate world hunger, cure disease, and vastly improve public health. However, these gene engineers have made it clear, through their business practices and political lobbying, that they intend to use GE to monopolize the global market for seeds, foods, fiber, and medical products.

Revolutionary "Frankenfood" Technology

GE is a revolutionary new technology that is still in its early experimental stages of development. This technology has the power to break down the natural genetic barriers—not only between species—but between humans, animals, and plants. Randomly inserting together the genes of non-related species—utilizing viruses, antibiotic-resistant genes, and bacteria as vectors, markers, and promoters—permanently alters their genetic codes.

GE products clearly have the potential to be toxic and a threat to human health.

The gene-altered organisms that are created pass these genetic changes onto their offspring through heredity. Gene engineers all over the world are now snipping, inserting, recombining, rearranging, editing, and programming genetic material. Animal genes and even human genes are randomly inserted into the chromosomes of plants, fish, and animals, creating heretofore unimaginable transgenic life forms. For the first time in history, transnational biotechnology corporations are becoming the architects and "owners" of life.

With little or no regulatory restraints, labeling requirements, or scientific protocol, bio-engineers have begun creating hundreds of new GE "Frankenfoods" and crops. The research is done with little concern for the human and environmental hazards and the negative socioeconomic impacts on the world's several billion farmers and rural villagers.

An increasing number of scientists are warning that current gene-splicing techniques are crude, inexact, and unpredictable—and therefore inherently dangerous. Yet, pro-biotech governments and regulatory agencies, led by the US, maintain that GE foods and crops are "substantially equivalent" to conventional foods, and therefore require neither mandatory labeling nor pre-market safety-testing.

Inherently Dangerous and Frightening

This Brave New World of Frankenfoods is frightening. There are currently more than four dozen GE foods and crops being grown or sold in the US. These foods and crops are widely dispersed into the food chain and the environment. Over 80 million acres of GE crops are presently under cultivation in the US, while up to 750,000 dairy cows are being injected regularly with Monsanto's recombinant Bovine Growth Hormone (rBGH). Most supermarket processed food items now "test positive" for the presence of GE ingredients. In addition, several dozen more GE crops are in the final stages of development and will soon be released into the environment and sold in the marketplace. The "hidden menu" of these unlabeled GE foods and food ingredients in the US now includes soybeans, soy oil, corn, potatoes, squash, canola oil, cottonseed oil, papaya, tomatoes, and dairy products.

GE food and fiber products are inherently unpredictable and dangerous—for humans, for animals, the environment, and for the future of sustainable and organic agriculture. As Dr. Michael Antoniou, a British molecular scientist points out, gene-splicing has already resulted in the "unexpected production of toxic substances . . . in genetically engineered bacteria, yeast, plants, and animals with the problem remaining undetected until a major health hazard has arisen." The hazards of GE foods and crops fall into three categories: human health hazards, environmental hazards, and socio-economic hazards. A brief look at the already-proven and likely hazards of GE products provides a convincing argument for why we need a global moratorium on all GE foods and crops.

Toxins and Poisons Created Through Genetic Engineering

GE products clearly have the potential to be toxic and a threat to human health. In 1989, a genetically engineered brand of L-tryptophan, a common dietary supplement, killed 37 Americans. More than 5,000 others were permanently disabled or afflicted with a potentially fatal and painful blood disorder, eosinophilia myalgia syndrome (EMS), before it was recalled by the Food and Drug Administration (FDA). The manufacturer, Showa Denko, Japan's third largest chemical company, had for the first time in 1988–89 used GE bacteria to produce the over-the-counter supplement. It is believed that the bacteria somehow became contaminated during the recombinant DNA process. Showa Denko has paid out over $2 billion in damages to EMS victims.

In 1999, front-page stories in the British press revealed Rowett Institute scientist Dr. Arpad Pusztai's explosive research findings that GE potatoes are poisonous to mammals. These potatoes were spliced with DNA from the snowdrop plant and a commonly used viral promoter, the Cauliflower Mosaic Virus (CaMv). GE snowdrop potatoes were found to be significantly different in chemical composition from regular potatoes, and when fed to lab rats, damaged their vital organs and immune systems. The damage to the rats' stomach linings apparently was a severe viral infection caused by the CaMv viral promoter apparently giving the rats a severe viral infection. Most alarming of all, the CaMv viral promoter is spliced into nearly all GE foods and crops.

Dr. Pusztai's path breaking research work unfortunately remains incomplete. Government funding was cut off and he was fired after he spoke to the media. More and more scientists around the world are warning that genetic manipulation can increase the levels of natural plant toxins or allergens in foods (or create entirely new toxins) in unexpected ways by switching on genes that produce poisons. Since regulatory agencies do not currently require the kind of thorough chemical and feeding tests that Dr. Pusztai was conducting, consumers have now become involuntary guinea pigs in a vast genetic experiment. Dr. Pusztai warns, "Think of William Tell shooting an arrow at a target. Now put a blindfold on the man doing the shooting and that's the reality of the genetic engineer doing a gene insertion".

People with food allergies ... may likely be harmed by exposure to foreign proteins spliced into common food products.

Genetic Engineering and Threats to Human Health

In 1994, the FDA approved the sale of Monsanto's controversial rBGH. This GE hormone is injected into dairy cows to force them to produce more milk. Scientists have warned that significantly higher levels (400–500% or more) of a potent chemical hormone, Insulin-Like Growth Factor (IGF-1), in the milk and dairy products of rBGH injected cows, could pose serious hazards such as human breast, prostate, and colon cancer. A number of studies have shown that humans with elevated levels of IGF-1 in their bodies are much more likely to get cancer. The US Congressional watchdog agency, the GAO [General Accounting Office], told the FDA not to approve rBGH. They argued that injecting the cows with rBGH caused higher rates of udder infections requiring increased antibiotic treatment. The increased use of antibiotics poses an unacceptable risk for public health. In 1998, Monsanto/FDA documents that had previously been withheld, were released by government scientists in Canada showing damage to laboratory rats fed dosages of rBGH. Significant infiltration of rBGH into the prostate of the rats as well as thyroid cysts indicated potential cancer hazards from the drug. Subsequently, the government of Canada banned rBGH in early 1999. The European Union (EU) has had a ban in place since 1994. Although rBGH continues to be injected into 10% of all US dairy cows, no other industrialized country has legalized its use. The GATT Codex Alimentarius, a United Nations food standards body, has refused to certify that rBGH is safe.

In 1996, a major GE food disaster was narrowly averted when Nebraska researchers learned that a Brazil nut gene spliced into soybeans could induce potentially fatal allergies in people sensitive to Brazil nuts. Animal tests of these Brazil nut-spliced soybeans had turned up negative. People with food allergies (which currently afflicts 8% of all American children), whose symptoms can range from mild unpleasantness to sudden death, may likely be harmed by exposure to foreign proteins spliced into common food products. Since humans have never before eaten most of the foreign proteins now being gene-spliced into foods, stringent pre-market safety-testing (including long-term animal feeding and volunteer human feeding studies) is necessary in order to prevent a future public health disaster.

Mandatory labeling is also necessary so that those suffering from food allergies can avoid hazardous GE foods and so that public health officials can trace allergens back to their source when GE-induced food allergies break out.

In fall 2001, public interest groups, including Friends of the Earth and the Organic Consumers Association, revealed that lab tests indicated that an illegal and likely allergenic variety of GE, Bt-spliced corn called StarLink, had been detected in Kraft Taco Bell shells, as well as many other brand name products. The StarLink controversy generated massive media coverage and resulted in the recall of hundreds of millions of dollars of food products and seeds.

Damage to Food Quality Nutrition and the Environment

A 1999 study by Dr. Marc Lappe published in the *Journal of Medicinal Food* found that concentrations of beneficial phytoestrogen compounds thought to protect against heart disease and cancer were lower in GE soybeans than in traditional strains. These and other studies, including Dr. Pusztai's, indicate that GE food will likely result in foods lower in quality and nutrition. For example, the milk from cows injected with rBGH contains higher levels of pus, bacteria, and fat.

When gene engineers splice a foreign gene into a plant or microbe, they often link it to another gene, called an antibiotic resistance marker gene (ARM), that helps determine if the first gene was successfully spliced into the host organism. Some researchers warn that these ARM genes might unexpectedly recombine with disease-causing bacteria or microbes in the environment or in the guts of animals or people who eat GE food.

These new combinations may be contributing to the growing public health danger of antibiotic resistance—of infections that cannot be cured with traditional antibiotics, for example new strains of salmonella, e-coli, campylobacter, and enterococci. German researchers have found antibiotic resistant bacteria in the guts of bees feeding on gene-altered rapeseed (canola) plants. EU [European Union] authorities are currently considering a ban on all GE foods containing antibiotic resistant marker genes.

Contrary to biotech industry propaganda, recent studies have found that US farmers growing GE crops are using just as many toxic pesticides and herbicides as conventional farmers and in some cases are using more. Crops genetically engineered to be herbicide-resistant account for almost 80% of all GE crops planted in 2000. The "benefits" of these herbicide-resistant crops are that farmers can spray as much of a particular herbicide on their crops as they want—killing the weeds without damaging their crop. Scientists estimate that herbicide-resistant crops planted around the globe will triple the amount of toxic broad-spectrum herbicides used in agriculture. These broad-spectrum herbicides are designed to literally kill everything green.

The leaders in biotechnology are the same giant chemical companies—Monsanto, DuPont, Aventis, and Syngenta (the merger between Novartis and Astra-Zeneca)—that sell toxic pesticides. The same companies that create the herbicide resistant GE plants are also selling the herbicides. The farmers are then paying for more herbicide treatment from the same companies that sold them the herbicide resistant GE seeds.

"Genetic pollution" and collateral damage from GE field crops already have begun to wreak environmental havoc. Wind, rain, birds, bees, and insect pollinators have begun carrying genetically-altered pollen into adjoining fields, polluting the DNA of crops of organic and non-GE farmers. An organic farm in Texas has been contaminated with genetic drift from GE crops grown on a nearby farm. EU regulators are considering setting an "allowable limit" for genetic contamination of non-GE foods, because they don't believe genetic pollution can be controlled.

Because they are alive, gene-altered crops are inherently more unpredictable than chemical pollutants—they can reproduce, migrate, and mutate. Once released, it is virtually impossible to recall GE organisms back to the laboratory or the field.

In 1999, Cornell University researchers made a startling discovery. They found that pollen from GE Bt corn was poisonous to Monarch butterflies. The study adds to a growing body of evidence that GE crops are adversely affecting a number of beneficial insects, including ladybugs and lacewings, as well as beneficial soil microorganisms, bees, and possibly birds.

Genetically engineering crops to be herbicide-resistant or to produce their own pesticide presents dangerous problems.

Pests and weeds will inevitably emerge that are pesticide or herbicide-resistant, which means that stronger, more toxic chemicals will be needed to get rid of the pests. Herbicide resistant "superweeds" are already emerging. GE crops such as rapeseed (canola) have spread their herbicide-resistance traits to related weeds such as wild mustard plants.

Gene-splicing will inevitably result in unanticipated outcomes and dangerous surprises that damage plants and the environment.

Lab and field tests also indicate that common plant pests such as cotton bollworms, living under constant pressure from GE crops, will soon evolve into "superpests" completely immune to Bt sprays and other environmentally sustainable biopesticides. This will present a serious danger for organic and sustainable fanners whose biological pest management practices will be unable to cope with increasing numbers of superpests and superweeds.

Gene-splicing will inevitably result in unanticipated outcomes and dangerous surprises that damage plants and the environment. Several years ago, researchers conducting experiments at Michigan State University found that genetically altering plants to resist viruses can cause the viruses to mutate into new, more virulent forms. Scientists in Oregon found that a GE soil microorganism, Klebsiella planticola, completely killed essential soil nutrients. Environmental Protection Agency whistle blowers issued similar warnings in 1997 protesting government approval of a GE soil bacterium called Rhizobium melitoli.

By virtue of their "superior" genes, some GE plants and animals will inevitably run amok, overpowering wild species in the same way that exotic species, such as kudzu vine and Dutch elm disease, have created problems when introduced in North America. What will happen to wild fish and marine species, for example, when scientists release into the environment carp, salmon, and trout that are twice as large, and eat twice as much food, as their wild counterparts?

Socioeconomic and Ethical Hazards of Genetic Engineering

The patenting of GE foods and widespread biotech food production threatens to eliminate farming as it has been practiced for 12,000 years. GE patents such as the Terminator Technology will render seeds infertile and force hundreds of millions of farmers who now save and share their seeds to purchase evermore-expensive GE seeds and chemical inputs from a handful of global biotech/seed monopolies. If the trend is not stopped, the patenting of transgenic plants and food-producing animals will soon lead to universal "bioserfdom" in which farmers will lease their plants and animals from biotech conglomerates such as Monsanto and pay royalties on seeds and offspring. Family and indigenous farmers will be driven off the land and consumers' food choices will be dictated by a cartel of transnational corporations. Rural communities will be devastated. Hundreds of millions of farmers and agricultural workers worldwide will lose their livelihoods.

The genetic engineering and patenting of animals reduces living beings to the status of manufactured products. A purely reductionist science, biotechnology reduces all life to bits of information (genetic code) that can be arranged and rearranged at whim. Stripped of their integrity and sacred qualities, animals that are merely objects to their "inventors" will be treated as such. Currently, hundreds of GE "freak" animals are awaiting patent approval from the federal government. One can only wonder, after the wholesale gene altering and patenting of animals, will GE "designer babies" be next?

2

Genetically Engineered Foods Have Not Been Proven to Be Harmful

Tracey Schelmetic

Tracey Schelmetic is a contributing editor for Technology Marketing Corporation (TMC), a marketing media company for communications and technology industries.

Supporters of genetically modified (GM) foods tout its benefits but critics call it Frankenfood that is unsafe to eat. The scientific evidence on the impact of GM food on human health is inconclusive, and while no evidence has been discovered so far showing that GM food is harmful, it is possible that ingesting GM food could have long term effects on health. Meanwhile, there is some evidence that GM crops are creating superweeds, that pests may be adapting to the toxins implanted into GM crops, and that GM crops may be affecting biodiversity. In the future, there will likely be a global fight over whether GM foods should be labeled, especially since a recent United Nations guideline on GM food now allows each country to require labeling without fear that they will be challenged for restricting free trade. In the end, if the public rejects GM food, it may not matter what science actually concludes about GM safety.

There are some topics that few people are able to sit in the middle of. The link or lack of link between vaccines and health threats is one. Genetically modified (GM) food is another.

Tracey Schelmetic, "Public Perception—Not Science—Will Rule the GM Food Debate," Thomas Net News, August 9, 2011. www.news.thomasnet.com. Copyright © 2011 by Thomas Publishing Company LLC. All rights reserved. Reproduced by permission.

GM food, according to the World Health Organization (WHO), is any foodstuff that contains "organisms in which the genetic material (DNA) has been altered in a way that does not occur naturally." GM food began appearing on store shelves in the early 1990s: primarily in the form of soybeans, corn, canola and cottonseed oil whose plants had been tinkered with genetically in order to introduce desirable traits: resistance to pests, herbicides or less-than-desirable weather and growing conditions, improved product shelf life, and increased nutritional value. Its proponents believe that it has the potential to save the world.

Its opponents, on the other hand, call it "Frankenfood." Describing the topic of GM food as "contentious" is a little like describing World War I as "a bit of a dust-up."

Potential Harm Versus Benefits

So maybe I should declare from the beginning that I am, in fact, one of those oddballs who sit in the middle of the GM food debate. While I admit that the idea of putting food into my body that has had its DNA fiddled with makes me uneasy: particularly since while most studies haven't found a "Eureka!" moment of definitive correlation between GM foods and harm to human health, reputable scientists still use language a little too cautious in their descriptions. Studies are still rife with conclusions such as, "there is no evidence so far that GM foods are harmful". This tells me that scientists are still hedging their bets, as if they do believe that there is feasibility for the scientific community to find, 10 or 20 years down the road, that such a negative correlation exists.

Here's an example: in early July [2011], Health Canada spokesperson Stephane Shank put forth this ringing endorsement for GM food: "To date, Health Canada has not identified health risks associated with GM foods that have been approved for sale in Canada."

To date. Which sounds a bit like, "It might be harmful, but we just haven't found that evidence yet. Bon appétit!"

On the flip side, I don't think anyone with a heart and some scientific intelligence could fail to recognize the benefits of, for example, grain that is modified to be able to grow in drought-prone regions, providing food for people who have none, or food crops that are resistant to common pests and plant diseases, increasing the crop yields and decreasing the chances of food shortages.

So far the studies looking for a direct connection between GM foods and negative human health consequences have come up with an inconclusive mixed bag of unsupported theories.

What I do know, after reading material from both sides, is that neither side is innocent of invoking soap-opera emotions and blatant propaganda to try and win coveted "hearts and minds" to their causes.

But as the plastics companies that resisted removing Bisphenol-A (BPA) from their products because science was on the fence about human health effects from ordinary exposure, it doesn't, in the end, matter what the scientists say if the public perception is strong enough. Swear your BPA-laden baby bottles are safe all you want, but if your customers go with their gut feelings and drop you to buy your competitors' BPA-free baby bottles, all you're left with is an empty argument and a sense of righteous indignation, which is hard to turn a profit on.

Scientists' Concerns About GM Foods

While so far the studies looking for a direct connection between GM foods and negative human health consequences have come up with an inconclusive mixed bag of unsupported theories, there are some other valid concerns.

While many GM crops are genetically adjusted to be resistant to pests—some plants can now actually put out small amounts of substances that are toxic to pests but harmless to humans—there is evidence that this is a short-term effect, and pests are actually adapting to the toxins the GM crops produce.

Research suggests that while genetically modified corn may produce toxins that are harmful to pests and harmless to humans, the monarch butterfly hasn't been so lucky.

A new study of corn genetically engineered to be resistant to the western corn rootworm has found that though the resistance is strong for the first year or two, subsequent generations of rootworms adapt to and become immune to the anti-pest properties.

While the study's authors do not recommend scrapping GM corn entirely, they do recommend rotating crops in fields so the bugs don't have several consecutive growing seasons to adapt to the pest resistance.

Others fear the impact of genetically modified crops on biodiversity. Research suggests that while genetically modified corn may produce toxins that are harmful to pests and harmless to humans, the monarch butterfly hasn't been so lucky. A new study has found a direct correlation between increasing acreage of GM corn in Mexico and decreasing populations of monarch butterflies, possibly because the GM corn is also toxic to milkweed, a host plant for the over-wintering butterflies.

Other scientists are concerned about another unintended consequence of GM crops: the development of so-called "superweeds."

Some genetically modified plants are created to be tolerant of intensive herbicides like Monsanto's Roundup, which is made of a chemical called glyphosate. These plants are referred to by farmers as being "Roundup Ready." Once the crop plants emerge, farmers can hit the fields with an intensive application of glyphosate to discourage the growth of unwelcome weeds without killing the soy or corn. Another unintended consequence of this practice, however, is the development of so-called "superweeds," or weeds that have quickly developed resistance to herbicides that then spread to non GM crops, making it harder for farmers to eradicate them.

Last year, it was estimated that as much as seven to 10 million acres of farm land in the U.S. is affected by superweeds, and the farmers in those areas are having to resort to even more toxic herbicides, plus old-fashioned hand removal of weeds in order to keep crops healthy: something that could potentially drive up food prices.

While natural mutations in plants and animals occur over millions of years and have a way of being self-correcting, any evolutionary biologist is going to be wary of sudden, artificial changes in the genetic makeup of any living thing: the unintended consequences are hard to predict and can often be far-reaching.

"The biotech industry is taking us into a more pesticide-dependent agriculture when they've always promised, and we need to be going in, the opposite direction," Bill Freese, a science policy analyst for the Center for Food Safety in Washington, told the *New York Times*.

Government Perceptions of GM Foods

While U.S. policy has generally been in favor of GM crops and the farmers that produce them, GM companies haven't been given a blank check, even in the U.S.

One recent example involves not crops, but genetically modified fish. In June [2011], a sub-committee within the U.S. House of Representatives voted to prevent the FDA [US

Food and Drug Administration] approval of a kind of fast-growing modified salmon developed by a company called AquaBounty Technologies.

Rep. Don Young—a Republican from Alaska—actually referred to the fish as "Frankenfish."

"Frankenfish is uncertain and unnecessary," said Young. "Should it receive approval as an animal drug, it clears the path to introduce it into the food supply. My amendment cuts them off before they can get that far. Any approval of genetically modified salmon could seriously threaten wild salmon populations as they grow twice as fast and require much more food."

Now . . . conventional wisdom says that when a Republican-controlled House comes out against your business, chances are pretty good you're in trouble on the regulatory and approval front.

Of course, it's important to note that the strongest opposition to the genetically engineered salmon came from state lawmakers in the Pacific Northwest. In addition to Rep. Young, Senators Lisa Murkowski (R-AK) and Patty Murray (D-WA) have also strongly come out against AquaBounty's fish.

So this begs the question: can the GM issue ever be discussed with not only unsupported gut emotions and personal feelings left out, but politics, too? If a drought-resistant grain could be modified to turn, for example, New Mexico and Arizona into breadbasket states like Iowa and Illinois, would politicians from the latter two states oppose that genetically modified grain in an attempt to protect their own states' economic interests?

I doubt even the the most politically optimistic person could answer "No" to that question.

In the case of AquaBounty's salmon, a lot of the opposition has been from the traditional salmon farm industry. The industry frets that if the bioengineered salmon is approved, it will be grown profitably in inland tanks, undermining other salmon production and giving AquaBounty a dominant position in the industry, reported the *New York Times.*

So is the objection to AquaBounty's fish more about genetic modification and its potential impact on human health and biodiversity, or eliminating competition? A little of both, obviously, but it's hard to figure out where one reason ends and the other begins.

GM Foods and Global Concerns

While ordinary Americans are only just starting to get a whiff of GM food views and politics, Europe is where the real public opinion against GM foods is strongest. EU [European Union] legislators voted in July to give each member state more autonomy over issues of genetically modified foodstuffs. Lawmakers agreed that individual EU governments should be free to ban the cultivation or import of GM crops based on environmental concerns, such as to protect biodiversity or prevent the spread of super weeds, reported *Reuters.*

The next few years will likely see an epic global fight over the labeling of GM products. Food companies that use GM products—and the farmers that grow GM crops—would prefer that there be no requirement for them to label the can of beans, the tofu or the cereal as containing GM ingredients: let the onus be on the organic food producers to use a label that proclaims "No GM ingredients" as a selling point to attract anti-GM customers.

On the flip side, environmentalists and anti-GM food activists would prefer that the requirement fall on the growers and producers of genetically modified food to wear the "Scarlet GM" label, so to speak, on their products. In this way, consumers could be confident that any product they purchase without a label is clear of GM ingredients.

While many European nations operate under the latter, more pro-consumer model, as of today, the U.S. FDA does not require food products containing GM ingredients to bear labels informing the customer of this if the GM products do not significantly change the nutritional value or allergen contents of the food, and nearly all FDA recommendations are "voluntary" at this time.

Maybe it's not going to matter what science finds about GM foods. If the public vetoes these ingredients from the food supply . . . will it really matter . . . whether they're safe or not?

But food production is a global concern, and in July, the United Nations issued a final decision on a Codex for international guidance on GM food labeling. The decision was the result of about 16 years of acrimonious fighting between pro-GM economies like the U.S. and Canada against more anti-GM countries like those in Europe, and environmental and consumer groups versus the genetically modified food industries.

Oddly enough, both sides claimed victory. While the UN Codex is just a series of "guidelines" (rather than mandates) for countries to follow for GM food labeling (this is where the food industries claim victory), the Codex also rules that a country's decision to implement mandatory labels on foods containing GM ingredients cannot be challenged by other nations as obstructions to existing free trade agreements (this is where the consumer groups and environmentalists are claiming victory).

What this does mean is that in countries that do mandate labeling of GM ingredients, consumers will be in a better position to choose whether they want to consume GM food at the point of the supermarket shelf. Those of us who live in countries without mandatory labeling will have to shop a little more carefully and do a little more research.

So in the end, maybe it's not going to matter what science finds about GM foods. If the public vetoes these ingredients from the food supply—by checking labels and purchasing accordingly, will it really matter, in the end, whether they're safe or not?

3

The Problems Caused by Genetically Engineered Foods Must Be Resolved

Divyahans Gupta

Divyahans Gupta is a student at Harker, a co-ed, non-sectarian independent school in San Jose, California.

Genetically modified (GM) crops have spread around the globe and grown rapidly in recent years because they promise many benefits. However, GM foods pose a real danger to human health, the environment, and the global economy. For example, GM foods are touted as increasing nutrition, but no one knows the long-term effects of consuming these foods. Scientists and others warn that this technology will cause higher levels of toxins, allergens, antibiotic resistance, immune suppression, and cancer. GM food production also threatens to deplete soils, spread uncontrollably, and cause permanent damage to the environment and biodiversity. In addition, since GM seeds are controlled by corporations, the emphasis is profit and these seeds often are too expensive for small farmers and have led to patent infringement lawsuits. If GM foods are going to be truly beneficial, solutions must be found for these problems.

More than ten million farmers planted 252 million acres of genetically-modified (GM) crops in 2006. From 1996 to 2000, acreage of GM crops globally increased 25-fold. The prevalence and rapid growth of GM crops are accredited to

Divyahans Gupta, "Food Frenzy: Growing Concerns Over Genetically Modified Foods," *Triple Helix Online*, January 26, 2011. www.triplehelixblog.com. Copyright © 2011 Triple Helix Online. All rights reserved. Reproduced by permission.

the benefits it provides. Biotechnology companies alter the DNA of crops, either by removing or inserting genes from other species, to alter the genetic makeup of the crop. Previously, farmers enhanced crops through breeding techniques. Today, scientists engineer plants to immunize them against viruses, herbicides, and pesticides, withstand inclement weather, increase nutritional value, and increase crop production. Some people hail GM foods as the solution to world hunger and other global issues; however, these foods pose a significant danger to our health, safety, global economy, and environment.

Health Benefits and Risks of GM Foods

Genetically-modified foods can decrease malnutrition in countries and fight world hunger. With the increase of yield, farmers could sell more crops to the world. Biotechnology companies alter the genetic make-up of crops to enhance their nutritional value with antioxidants and vitamins. For example, scientists at the Swiss Federal Institute of Technology Institute for Plant Sciences modified a rice strain with an increased amount of vitamin A from daffodils. The malnourished in developing countries can obtain more nutrients through GM foods as the enhanced nutritional value and high yield of these crops can be extremely beneficial to countries where food is scarce. In addition, vaccines can be inserted into GM foods as scientists have already implanted a highly effective Hepatitis B vaccine into edible plants for third world countries. This could prevent diseases and viruses from spreading in developing countries. Thus, GM foods provide a solution to many of today's global problems.

Though GM foods are modified to increase nutrition, the long-term effects are unknown. The Center for Food Safety states that the consumption of GM foods may lead to "higher risks of toxicity, allergenicity, antibiotic resistance, immune-suppression, and cancer." After a Japanese chemical company,

Showa Denko, introduced L-tryptophan, a genetically-modified, over-the-counter dietary supplement, 37 Americans died in 1989 of Eosinophilia Myalgia Syndrome upon consuming it. In 1999, studies done by the renowned scientist Dr. Arpad Putzai, revealed that the Cauliflower Mosaic Virus, a promoter that helps transcribe new genes, was the most likely cause of the organ damage and viral infections in rats that were fed potatoes with the promoter. Putzai emphasized that GM foods do not undergo sufficient testing before they are sold, and advised people to beware of GM foods on a British television program. In addition, he argued that the long-term effects of GM foods might be harmful upon discovering that the rats experienced the ill-effects after a time corresponding to ten human years. Dr. Putzai's research was met with a fierce backlash from biotechnology companies because the report exposed risks related with their products. These studies indicate that GM organisms often produce unintended, and sometimes fatal, effects.

When inserting a gene into an organism, scientists introduce the gene with an antibiotic resistance marker that helps determine if the inserted gene is successfully implemented. Some scientists warn that immunizing organisms against viruses with antibiotics will carry over to an antibiotic resistance to bacteria, thus creating an antibiotic-resistant bacterium. Also, some people fear that the consumption of GM foods may cause allergic reactions. For instance, if a gene from a peanut is introduced in a banana, then consumption of the banana may cause an allergic reaction. Cross-contamination between two crops could also trigger allergic reactions in some humans that consume it. One such disaster was avoided in 1996, when a company proposed to insert a gene from a Brazil nut into soybean. A group of researchers in Nebraska notified the company that the new strain could have ill-effects on some humans with allergies, even though the company had claimed that the strain had no ill-effects during their animal testing.

In the United States, the Food and Drug Administration (FDA) labels GM foods as GRAS (Genetically Recognized As Safe). In other words, the FDA believes that GM foods are not different than non-GM foods. Thus, no additional evaluation or labeling is necessary for GM foods before their distribution. However, consumer organizations argue that GM foods need labeling. Additionally, the health hazards of GM foods are mostly unknown because biotechnology companies do not allow independent researchers to publish studies done on GM seeds. In order to obtain the seeds, scientists must sign an agreement to only publish studies in peer-review journals that have been approved by the company. These companies essentially produce consumer propaganda, putting public health at risk. Thus, the health and safety risks associated with GM foods are significant enough to prevent it from becoming the solution to global problems and must be assessed.

Instead of benefitting a farm, GM foods can destroy one.

GM Foods and the Environment

GM foods can reduce the need for chemical use if pesticides are fused into the crops. Decreasing the use of pesticides and herbicides prevents agricultural waste run-off. Monsanto, a biotechnology company, developed soybeans resistant to a certain herbicide. Thus, farmers can save money since they need to apply the herbicide only once to eliminate weeds. As a result, GM foods can reduce the use of pesticides and the residual pesticide levels in the environment, which prevents water contamination and decreasing biodiversity. Thus, GM foods can positively affect the environment.

However, the production of GM foods inflates a variety of environmental concerns. GM crops can be so productive that they can overwork the soil and require vast amounts of resources, like water, to survive. GM crops can also become pests if they grow uncontrollably. In land where space is limited, the uncontrollable GM crop could spread over other crops and decrease biodiversity. By [naturalist Charles] Darwin's theory of natural selection, crops that are genetically modified to resist herbicides and pesticides would create "superbugs" and "superweeds" that are immune to any toxic chemicals. Even if a pesticide or herbicide is made, it is probable that the toxin would kill beneficial insects, like bees, and hurt the soil. Cross-contamination between GM crops and weeds can also create unmanageable weeds and bugs. Indeed, instead of benefitting a farm, GM foods can destroy one.

The introduction of GM plants may have negative effects on plant-dependent insects. Corn that was genetically modified to resist the pesticide, Bacillus Thuringiensis [Bt], caused death among monarch butterflies that fed from milkweeds mat caught the corn's pollen. Studies have shown that GM foods cause various health ailments in animals, such as stomach-lining erosion and dramatic changes in body weight. Therefore, GM crops can directly and indirectly affect animals and plants and can destroy agriculture from an environmental standpoint. The negative effects that GM crops have on the environment are equally as important as the potential benefits.

For GM foods to be more beneficial, solutions to the health, safety, economical, and environmental problems must be addressed.

The Economy and Politics

Though GM foods can boost the agricultural economy, they can also have negative impacts. Since biotechnology companies are often monopolies, the price of seeds could extend beyond the reach of farmers. Small farmers in developing countries are tempted to purchase GM seeds because of their numerous benefits. However, purchasing GM seeds makes them dependent on the companies. This destabilizes local economies because farmers will have to increase the price of their crops to compensate for the high price of the seeds. Furthermore, biotechnology companies might gain too much control over crop production in developing countries and hinder their growth in the future.

There have been patent disputes between biotechnology companies and farmers. Farmers have been accused of patent infringement for cultivating crops that cross-pollinated with GM crops. Monsanto, a biotechnology company, proposed to invest in genetic use restriction technology (GURT). V-GURT, a type of GURT, produces GM seeds that become sterile after one harvest. Though it prevents cross-pollination of regular and GM crops, this technology would make farmers completely dependent on biotechnology companies. In addition, farmers often store seeds from previous harvests for the next year. However, with V-GURT, farmers would have to purchase seeds from biotechnology companies annually, creating an enormous financial burden for them. After a long debate, Monsanto agreed to end its research on V-GURT. Still, biotechnology companies seem more interested in profiting than participating in a global solution.

Though GM foods may solve many global issues, there are obstacles that need to be overcome before they can be commercially produced. Otherwise, the production of GM foods will result in a multitude of problems. Additionally, the malevolence of biotechnology companies makes resolving these obstacles difficult. For GM foods to be more beneficial, solutions to the health, safety, economical, and environmental problems must be addressed.

4

Genetically Engineered Foods Should Be Labeled

Jessica Emerson

Jessica Emerson is a writer for The Santa Fe New Mexican.

The debate about genetically modified (GM) crops should be focused on how these foods are being forced onto an unsuspecting public. According to a 2001 US Food and Drug Administration report, virtually all participants surveyed in a focus group want GM foods to be labeled. To date there is still no mandatory labeling for genetically engineered food. Serious human health problems, such as allergies, have increased since the introduction of GM crops and some animals have even died from consuming GM foods. Allowing biotech companies to freely market GM foods, threaten organic food production, and dominate seed production violates consumers' freedom of choice.

Grass-root seed and food conferences are springing up everywhere, it seems, and there is a common thread woven through each one—genetically modified organisms, or GMOs.

We have had several such conferences in Northern New Mexico: San Ildefonso and Santa Clara pueblos partnered for a spring conference and seed exchange; the Dixon Community Seed Exchange met in April.

Along with the agricultural experts talking about how to propagate and save traditional seeds at the 3rd annual symposium for Sustainable Food and Seed Sovereignty held at

Tesuque Pueblo in late September, was longtime canola farmer Percy Schmeiser, who fought the agri-business company Monsanto all the way to the Canadian Supreme Court. (Monsanto had sued Schmeiser for patent infringement because the company found its herbicide-resistant canola growing in Schmeiser's field; Schmeiser said the seed had blown there and counter-sued Monsanto for not preventing its genetically modified seed from contaminating his fields.)

Genetic modification of seeds, such as those that invaded Schmeiser's fields, involves the splicing of genes—from plant, human or nonhuman sources—into the DNA of a plant. The new life forms are called transgenic, genetically modified, genetically engineered or genetically modified organisms. . . .

Labeling Genetically Engineered Food

In February 2001, the U.S. Food and Drug Administration released a report that showed that "virtually all participants surveyed in focus groups want labeling." To date, there is still no mandatory labeling required for GE products.

Most genetically modified products carry fully functioning antibiotic-resistant genes—used as "selectable markers." According to a 1999 article in *The Journal* (Newcastle, UK), the presence of these antibiotic-resistant genes in a plant indicate that the organism has been successfully engineered.

Transgenic cotton contains Bromorynil (brand name Buctril), which causes birth defects and is suspected as a cause of liver tumors.

In an Internet posting, The Union of Concerned Scientists says that "eating these foods could reduce the effectiveness of antibiotics to fight disease." Hospitals around the world have increased incidences of infections from Methicillin-resistant Staphylococcus aureus, or MRSA. This organism has mutated and cannot be killed by most antibiotics. According to the

Center for Disease Control and Prevention, more than 90,000 Americans a year get deadly infections from MRSA. In 2005 the CDC reported 18,650 deaths associated with MRSA infections. Do we need more antibiotic-resistant organisms? . . .

Studies indicate that 2 percent of adults and 8 percent of children have food allergies. Inhaling pollen from GM crops is creating new threats that need to be researched and evaluated. In a 1999 statement posted on *Soy Info Online,* Joe Cummins, professor emeritus of genetics at the University of Western Ontario says that "GM pollen is likely to open an extended range of allergy and may cause autoimmune disease or other kinds of toxicity."

Studies indicate that residues of glyphosate in foods may increase the incidence of certain cancers, including non-Hodgkin's lymphoma. Bovine growth hormone (rBGH) found in most milk (unless the package notes otherwise) has been linked to breast cancer and diabetes. Transgenic cotton contains Bromorynil (brand name Buctril), which causes birth defects and is suspected as a cause of liver tumors. Cottonseed oil is found in many food products—another reason to read labels. Dr. Andre Menache, an official with the Israeli Ministry of Health warns that genetically engineered pigs, a common source for human organ transplants, may carry viruses that are potentially lethal.

It took 60 years of Dichloro-Diphenyl-Trichloroethane (or DDT) use for its health hazards to be recognized by the government and for it to be banned in the United States. (Thank you, Rachel Carson.)

Right to Know

Prince Charles of Great Britain is an outspoken anti-GE advocate. Who will speak for Americans?

The U.S. Food and Drug Administration consistently maintains that GE foods are safe. Margaret Miller, former lab supervisor for Monsanto, helped the company develop rBGH.

She left the company to become the deputy director of Human Food Safety and Consultation services at the FDA, where she helped streamline FDA approval for rBGH.

Consumers are calling for more safety guidelines. In January 2001, the Consumer Federation of America, a coalition of 270 consumer groups—including the American Association of Retired People—called on President George W. Bush and Congress to label biotech food and to require strict safety and environmental testing. In a 250-page report financed by a grant from the prestigious Rockefeller Foundation, the federation said the United States government has basically abandoned its responsibility to ensure the safety of genetically engineered foods. The report also calls for the end of a government policy that holds that GE foods are substantially equivalent to their non-GE counterparts.

Some politicians are speaking out. When he introduced the Genetically Engineered Food Right To Know Bill in 2001, Congressman Dennis Kucinich, D-Ohio, noted that "Government has a moral and legal responsibility to ensure the safety and purity of our food supply. We cannot abdicate this responsibility to global corporations whose goals may be limited to profit-making."

Congressman Jack Metcalf, R-Wash., joined Kucinich and a bipartisan group to cosponsor HR 3883, the GE Safety Testing Bill. He has been quoted as saying, "I am not convinced that enough research has been conducted to determine the long-term health effects of genetically modified foods, and I believe that American citizens should have the right to know what they are eating." . . .

We don't know the long-term effects of eating transgenic food. Do we want to be guinea pigs for biotech researchers? How will this affect our children, our grandchildren and the human race?

We do not know the long-term consequences of GM plants breeding with native plants. By the time we find out, there may be no biodiversity left on our planet: all food crops may depend on a few seed companies. It has been said that those who control food production control Earth.

5

Labels for Genetically Engineered Foods Are Not Necessary

Washington Post

The Washington Post *is a prominent daily newspaper published in Washington, DC.*

The US Food and Drug Administration is considering whether to allow genetically engineered (GE) salmon to be marketed. Scientific studies indicate that the salmon is no different from wild salmon, but consumer groups are demanding it be labeled, which could scare off consumers by implying that there is something wrong with GE fish. The US Food and Drug Administration (FDA) rules say that if genetically engineered foods are not materially different from natural products, they should not be labeled and these rules are properly based on safety and nutrition rather than on how a product is produced. The rules also allow producers of natural salmon to advertise that information. The FDA, therefore, is right to base its decision on science, not fear.

If a genetically engineered salmon is cleared for America's supermarkets, it will be because of convincing evidence the fish is safe to eat and not harmful to the environment. Scientific review to date shows the fish to be indistinguishable from its traditional counterpart. So demands that the altered fish be required to carry a government label seem to be more an attempt to scare off consumers than an effort to provide necessary health or nutritional information. Clearly, there must be caution in approving the first genetically altered animal for human consumption, but government regulators should stick to their long-held, sensible rules about what information must be disclosed for the public good.

No Reason to Label

The Food and Drug Administration [FDA] is considering whether to approve a fast-growing salmon developed over the past two decades by a biotech company from Massachusetts. The AquAdvantage salmon has been modified to include a gene from the Chinook salmon and DNA from an eel-like fish so that it grows twice as fast as conventional salmon. The FDA recently concluded two days of public hearings, and the expectation—based on data showing that the salmon pose no risks to humans or the environment—is that it's just a matter of time before the fish will be marketed. What has emerged as the hot-button issue, as *The [Washington] Post*'s Lyndsey Layton reported, is labeling and the implications of that for other genetically engineered animal products likely to follow.

A number of consumer groups pushing for mandatory labeling say that people have a right to know if the food they are eating comes from products that have been genetically modified. The not-so-subtle suggestion, of course, is that there is something different—or even wrong—with genetically modified food products, despite the science showing otherwise. The FDA's own rules say that once it is determined that a genetically modified food is not "materially significant" from naturally derived products, there is no reason to label it differently. Products from genetically modified crops, long permitted, do not carry special labels, nor does milk from cows given a growth hormone to produce more milk.

The food labeling rules, which have been tested in the courts, are properly focused on safety and nutrition and not on aspects of production such as, say, whether the product is the result of artificial insemination or cross breeding. Voluntary labeling is allowed as long as it is not false or misleading, so producers of conventionally raised salmon can publicize that fact as long as they do so truthfully. Public comment is still being accepted by FDA officials, who say that they will study the record before issuing a ruling. They are right to be careful and to base their decision on proven facts, not unfounded fears.

6

Genetically Engineered Foods Are Needed to Feed the World

A'ndrea Elyse Messer

A'ndrea Elyse Messer is the senior science and research information officer at Pennsylvania State University.

Providing enough food to feed a world population of nine billion—the expected future population—will require agriculture to do a better job of using nutrients, water, and energy, while reducing pollution. This means adapting crops to flourish at higher temperatures, with less water, and in salty soils. Genetically modified (GM) plants meeting these requirements would help to solve future food problems because after a decade of GM crops, there is no evidence of detrimental impacts or that GM crops are any different from crops modified by other techniques. Yet people in many countries still oppose the use of GM technology. This view might have to change if humans are to meet the challenge of feeding the world in the 21st century.

An integrated approach across multiple international disciplines is the only thing that can successfully solve the world's food problems while reducing pollution.

Efficient Use of Resources

"Using resources more efficiently is what it will take to put agriculture on a path to feed the expected future population of

A'ndrea Elyse Messer, "Global Effort Needed to Feed the World," Futurity.org, February 2011. Copyright © 2011 by Futurity.org. All rights reserved. Reproduced by permission.

nine billion people," says Nina Fedoroff, professor of biology and life sciences at Penn State [Pennsylvania State University].

"We especially need to do a better job using the nutrients, water, and energy needed to produce food."

Integrating various sectors of agriculture is one way to conserve and recycle resources, Federoff says. Using wastewater from freshwater aquiculture or fish ponds to irrigate and fertilize fruit and vegetables in a greenhouse and returning the cleaner water to the pond keeps the excess nutrients out of the groundwater, cleans the pond, and provides plants nutrients.

"We should ask how we can grow food with a minimum of water, maximum of renewable energy, and closest to where people are living," Fedoroff says.

Fedoroff presented her findings at the annual meeting of the American Association for the Advancement of Science in Washington, D.C.

[Professor Nina] Fedoroff suggests genetically modifying salt-tolerant plants to provide crops to grow in areas that are currently unused or underused.

"We need to expand our ability to farm on land not considered farmable because it is eroded or desertified, using water not considered suitable for farming because it is wastewater or saltwater," she says.

"We need to adapt current crops to higher temperatures and less water and we need to domesticate plants that have evolved to grow at high temperatures and in salty soils."

Some of the land currently considered useless has high soil salt content. Many plants already live in these areas, but few are domesticated.

Various wild types of Salicornia—a plant that grows on beaches and in salt marshes—are currently in use. One type of Salicornia popular in Europe, known as sea asparagus or sea bean, is eaten as a vegetable and its seeds contain about 30 percent edible oil, more than soy beans.

Salt marsh sheep, prized in France and gaining popularity in England, graze in coastal areas where salt-tolerant plants thrive. In Australia, saltbush mutton comes from sheep grazed on saltbush—Atriplex. However, salt-tolerant plants have not been domesticated.

From a human viewpoint, seeds are perhaps the most valuable plant parts, but many wild plants have seeds that, once ripe, fall from the plant. This works well for the wild plants but makes harvesting the seeds for replanting or consumption difficult.

"One of the first things in domestication is that plants are chosen that retain their seeds and do not experience seed shatter," Fedoroff says. "As a result of decades of genetic and genomic analysis, we gave a good idea of the genetic changes involved in domestication."

The Value of GMOs

Fedoroff suggests genetically modifying salt-tolerant plants to provide crops to grow in areas that are currently unused or underused. Currently, the expense of complying with government regulations applied to genetically modified organisms (GMOs) restricts development of plants to large companies producing commodity crops like cotton, corn, soy, and canola.

"Everything is reviewed on a case by case basis and it takes years and millions of dollars to get a single GMO out to farmers," says Fedoroff. "The expense of complying with the regulations has virtually eliminated the academic and public sectors from developing specialty crops, like fruits and vegetables, for farmers. Right now, the pipeline for producing of such crops is empty."

In the U.S., the Environmental Protection Agency regulates insect resistant GMOs with the same laws that they regulate fungicides and rodenticides—regulations that haven't changed since 1986, even though insect resistant GMO crops have decreased the use of insecticides almost 10 percent worldwide.

Also, genetically modified corn has lower levels of fungal toxins than conventional corn because it is resistant to boring insects that make holes through which fungi can enter the plant.

Evidence is growing that not only are there not any deleterious effects from insect-resistant and herbicide-tolerant GM plants, but that they are better for the environment because of decreased use of insecticides and less plowing.

"The most heartbreaking case is that of Golden Rice, which has been ready for 10 years, but is held up by the years of testing required by the regulations in many countries," says Fedoroff.

Genetically modified Golden Rice produces beta carotene, the naturally occurring precursor to vitamin A. Vitamin A deficiency is a problem in many underdeveloped countries and causes blindness and increased susceptibility to infections.

Rice is the most important staple food for large portions of the underdeveloped world.

"Evidence is growing that not only are there not any deleterious effects from insect-resistant and herbicide-tolerant GM plants, but that they are better for the environment because of decreased use of insecticides and less plowing," Fedoroff says.

A 2010 report recently published by the European Union on GMO safety research over the past 10 years concluded that GMO crops are not different from crops modified by other techniques. Yet GMO crops are the only ones regulated by governments.

"Meeting the food needs of a still-growing human and domestic animal population with less water while preserving remaining biodiversity is, arguably, the most profound challenge of the 21st century," says Fedoroff.

"And yet, in the face of overwhelming evidence of positive economic, agronomic and ecological impacts and the absence of detrimental impacts, people in many countries remain adamantly opposed to genetically modified organisms."

7

Genetically Engineered Crops Will Not Feed the World

Food & Water Watch

Food & Water Watch is a non-profit organization that advocates for public policies that support access to healthy, safe food and water around the world.

The biotech industry often claims that genetically engineered (GE) crops will help agriculture become more sustainable and help to feed the hungry world. In truth, most GE crops are designed to allow the use of more herbicides (such as Monsanto's Roundup) and have helped to create herbicide-resistant weeds, which causes farmers to use more toxic herbicides, not less. Also, studies have shown that GE crops do not produce higher crop yields; organic farming methods have had higher yield gains than GE methods. And so far, the biotech industry has failed to develop high-yield or drought-tolerant GE crops. GE crops and seeds really benefit only a few huge biotech companies that zealously protect their patents and profits. High-priced GE seeds and crops do not help small farmers in developing countries and they are not the answer to the challenge of how to feed the world's growing population.

Monsanto advertises that biotech crops can feed the world "from a raindrop," suggesting that GE [genetically engineered] crops are especially climate change resistant. In 2011, Roger Beachy, then-director of the U.S. Department of

Agriculture's primary research agency, the National Institute of Food and Agriculture, suggested to *Scientific American* magazine that GE crops protect traditional small farmers by reducing the need for agrochemicals. But this greenwashing doesn't change what is just agribusiness as usual: more agrochemicals, more fossil fuels and more intensive agricultural production.

Biotech Crops Do Not Reduce Agrochemical Use

Most GE crops are designed to be tolerant of specially tailored herbicides (mostly glyphosate, known as Roundup). Farmers can spray the herbicide on their fields, killing the weeds without harming their crops. Monsanto's herbicide-tolerant ("Roundup Ready") corn, soybeans and cotton were planted on 150 million U.S. acres in 2009. Glyphosate use on these Roundup Ready crops has grown steadily. Between 2001 and 2007, annual glyphosate use doubled to 185 million pounds. Glyphosate can pose risks to animals and the environment. A 2010 *Chemical Research in Toxicology* study found that glyphosate-based herbicides caused highly abnormal deformities and neurological problems in vertebrates. Another study found that glyphosate caused DNA damage to human cells even at lower exposure levels than recommended by the herbicide's manufacturer.

Biotech companies have focused on developing crops that are designed to work with the herbicides they sell, not on developing high-yield seeds.

Ubiquitous Roundup application has spawned glyphosate-resistant weeds, which drives farmers to apply more toxic herbicides and reduce conservation tilling, according to a 2010 National Research Council report. At least 15 weed species worldwide are resistant to glyphosate, including aggressive weeds like ragweed, mare's tail and water-hemp. Even the bio-tech company Syngenta predicts that glyphosate-resistant weeds will infest one-fourth of U.S. cropland by 2013.

Agricultural experts warn that these "superweeds" can lower farm yields, increase pollution and raise costs for farm-ers. Farmers may resort to other herbicides to combat super-weeds, including 2,4-D (an Agent Orange component) and atrazine, which have associated health risks, including endo-crine disruption and developmental abnormalities. Moreover, as glyphosate-resistant weeds strangle cropland, farmers have returned to deep tilling for weed management, abandoning tillage practices designed to slow soil erosion.

Biotech Crops Only Benefit Biotech Companies

Biotech companies have focused on developing crops that are designed to work with the herbicides they sell, not on devel-oping high-yield seeds. A 2009 Union of Concerned Scientists survey found that herbicide-tolerant corn and soybeans had no yield increase over non-GE crops, and insect-resistant corn had only a slight advantage over conventional corn. A 2001 University of Nebraska study found that conventional soy-beans had 5 to 10 percent higher yields than herbicide-tolerant soybeans.

A 2006 *Environmental Science and Technology* study found that low-input farms in developing countries had significant yield gains. A 2007 University of Michigan study found that organic farming in the developing world had higher yield gains than conventional production and could feed the global population without increasing the amount of cultivated land.

No Drought Protection

Biotech firms have promised high-yield and drought-resistant GE seeds, but these traits are not presently commercially available. The research has yet to achieve the complex interactions between genes necessary to endure environmental stressors such as drought.

Traditional breeding methods for stress tolerance are more resilient to disruption and climate change than GE crops because they complement and thrive in nutrient-rich and biodiverse soil. Even if research succeeded in developing drought-tolerant crops, biotechnology companies would control any viable seeds, potentially putting new seeds out of reach for poor countries.

The high costs for seeds and chemicals, uncertain yields, and potential to undermine local food security makes biotechnology a poor choice for the developing world

---

Only a few chemical and pharmaceutical giants dominate the seed industry, which once relied on universities for most research. By 2009, nearly all (93 percent) U.S. soybeans and four-fifths (80 percent) of corn cultivated were grown from seeds covered by Monsanto patents.

Biotech corn seed prices increased 9 percent annually between 2002 and 2008; soybean seed prices rose 7 percent annually. By 2009, Roundup Ready soybean seeds cost twice as much as conventional seeds.

Biotech companies also zealously pursue farmers that allegedly violate their patents. By 2007, Monsanto had filed 112 lawsuits against U.S. farmers for patent infringement, recovering between $85.7 and $160.6 million. In the developing world, patented GE seeds threaten the traditional practice of saving and sharing seeds from harvested crops to plant the next season.

GE Crops Will Not Feed a Hungry Planet

High-priced seeds and herbicides are ill-suited to farmers in the developing world. The prestigious 2009 International Assessment of Agriculture Knowledge, Science and Technology for Development concluded that the high costs for seeds and chemicals, uncertain yields, and potential to undermine local food security makes biotechnology a poor choice for the developing world.

For example, Indian farmers, wooed by Monsanto's marketing have widely adopted GE cotton. Farmers take out high-interest loans to afford the GE seeds, which can be twice as expensive as conventional seeds. Half the pesticides in India are applied to cotton. Some farmers significantly over-apply these chemicals, making agricultural workers highly vulnerable to health problems. More than half of farmers lack access to irrigation and are dependent on a punctual rainy season for a good crop. And when GE cotton crops fail, farmers are often unable to repay the substantial debt. The steeper treadmill of debt with GE crops contributes to a rising number of farmer suicides in India—exceeding 17,000 in 2009.

Despite their huge public relations campaigns, biotechnology is not solving our sustainability problems—it's making them worse and creating more.

8

Genetically Engineered Foods Threaten to Contaminate Organic Food

Paula Crossfield

Paula Crossfield is the co-founder and managing editor of Civil Eats, a food policy site that promotes sustainability. She also is a contributing producer at The Leonard Lopate Show *on New York Public Radio, where she focuses on food issues.*

Recent decisions by the US Department of Agriculture to allow genetically modified (GM) sugar beets and alfalfa increase the risk that organic foods will be contaminated by GM material. Despite proposals to protect organic crops from GM seeds, it is impossible for these two farming methods to co-exist because there are many ways for contamination to occur. Further, since GM seeds are patented by biotechnology companies, these companies have the legal right to sue organic farmers whose crops become contaminated by GM traits. This regulatory stance places the burden on organic farmers to test for and prevent contamination, resulting in higher prices for organic food, and threatening the future of organic farming.

Last Friday [February 4, 2011], the USDA [US Department of Agriculture] announced the partial deregulation of genetically modified sugar beets, defying a court order to complete an Environmental Impact Statement (EIS) in advance of a decision. This move follows on the heels of the full deregulation late last month of genetically modified (GM) alfalfa, the fourth most common row crop in the United States, which is most often used as feed for cattle.

If you eat beef, or take milk and sugar in your coffee (and even if you don't), here is why you should care: The move could put organic foods at risk for contamination and make it more expensive.

Co-existence Between GM and Organic Farmers Not Possible

Secretary of Agriculture Tom Vilsack has attempted to stave off further litigation and quell the mounting antagonism between farmers growing GM seed and organic farmers by proposing "co-existence" between the two.

Part of Vilsack's plan for co-existence includes using buffers between organic and GM fields and even placing geographic restrictions on the growth of GM seeds. This is the first time such a discussion had been broached by the USDA. New York University professor and food movement leader Marion Nestle called the move a "breakthrough," and we also ran an op-ed pushing for co-existence as the lesser of two evils. . . .

Aside from the transfer of genetic material through pollen, there are many other ways in which it has proven impossible to contain the risk of contamination.

But Vilsack's co-existence plan seemed to put President [Barack] Obama's pro-business agenda at risk. In fact, David Axelrod put the kibosh on the idea with a bad pun, encouraging "everyone to 'plow forward' on a plan for genetically produced alfalfa," according to Maureen Dowd.

Monsanto, the company behind 95 percent of GM sugarbeet seed and all of the GM alfalfa seed, had fought against the deal behind closed doors.

Worries were expressed about our biotech credibility abroad should we discuss any fallibility at home. But in a nod toward co-existence, Monsanto spokesman Tom Helscher told the AP [Associated Press], on Monday, "Since the advent of biotech crops, both biotech and organic production have flourished. We have no reason to think that will not continue to be the case." What Monsanto execs don't mention publicly is that co-existence is not possible, and as patent holders to the gene traits in their GM seeds, they have the right to sue farmers whose fields become contaminated by these traits.

"Certainly, on a commercial-scale crop, over time, you are going to get contamination," said Doug Gurian-Sherman, senior scientist at the Union of Concerned Scientists. "The provisions [in the EIS] will certainly reduce contamination, and they may delay it to some extent, but they're not going to prevent it."

American consumers want to know what they are eating, but the industry doesn't want to be forthcoming because letting the market decide would mean resistance to GM foods.

Aside from the transfer of genetic material through pollen, there are many other ways in which it has proven impossible to contain the risk of contamination. And unfortunately, there are plenty of real examples in which contamination has already happened.

There are well-documented cases with papaya in Hawaii, corn in Mexico, canola most recently in North Dakota, and creeping bentgrass, which pollinated grasses 13 miles away in Oregon. A test plot of a GM rice was even responsible for contaminating long grain varieties in five states in 2006, five years after Bayer CropScience had abandoned trials of its LL601 rice, costing the industry $2 billion.

In 1999, a corn variety called StarLink—which was not approved for human consumption—contaminated half of the Iowa corn harvest. Whether batches of corn meant for animal consumption were mixed with corn for human consumption on accident or through crops—pollination—we will never know exactly what happened. What we do know is that our current regulatory process has significant—in many cases, insurmountable—problems, and the concept of co-existence is merely a smoke screen that will create more of the same.

Implications for Organic Farmers

This is why deregulation has huge implications for organic farmers as well as consumers. The USDA does not test for contamination after deregulating a biotech crop. In the StarLink case, it was a non-profit group that found traces of the corn in taco shells. This means that the impetus will be on organic farmers to test their own crops, further increasing food prices. Worse, organic food could become more limited in availability if contamination becomes a widespread issue.

"Today, there are many committed consumers who want to know their farmer, feed their families wholesome dairy products, and be assured that their food isn't contaminated by GMOs," said Albert Straus, an organic dairy farmer from California who has spoken out against GM alfalfa. "If the organic feed supply for dairy cattle is contaminated with GMOs, farmers will no longer be able to offer truly organic milk to consumers, and everything we have worked to build will be compromised." Straus Family Creamery has been voluntarily testing its feed for GMOs since 2006, and carries the Non-GMO Project Seal on its label.

In addition, organic farmers fear economic loses in export markets—places like the European Union [EU] and Japan, where products containing traces of GM foods are consistently rejected. In addition to risks in the field, it is not uncommon for organic crops to be transported in rail cars, on boats and in truck beds where GM or conventional crops have also been transported. This means that a crop that has been tested by the farmer can still be contaminated later. With no protections in place, the organic farmer bears the majority of the risk.

The reason Japanese and EU consumers are driving the purity tests on crops coming from America is simple: When GM foods are sold in places like the EU or Japan, they are labeled as such. And this really is the critical issue. American consumers want to know what they are eating, but the industry doesn't want to be forthcoming because letting the market decide would mean resistance to GM foods.

"We don't challenge consumers on whether they want a red car or a blue car," said Gurian-Sherman. "But when it comes to choosing what they want to eat, the people that are supporting this technology seem to be greatly offended that the market in Europe and other places is doing what markets are suppose to do."

Letting the market decide would also mean more support for organics, which would force the USDA to protect that market-and thus our food supply-more conscientiously. Therefore, pushing for transparent labeling on food containing GMOs could be the first step in protecting our food supply from genetic contamination.

This will not be the last battle fought to preserve an agricultural product from contamination. In fact, any day now the FDA will be issuing a ruling about the first genetically altered animal—the GM salmon.

9

Genetically Engineered Crops Do Not Threaten Organic Food Production

Dick Taverne

Dick Taverne is the founder of Sense About Science, an independent charitable trust based in London that promotes a science-based approach to genetically engineered foods and other public issues.

The United States, unlike Europe, has allowed the cultivation of genetically modified (GM) crops for over a decade, but that policy is now under fire from anti-GM activists and organic farmers who have pressured the US Department of Agriculture to limit where GM crops can be planted to avoid contamination of organic crops. This assault on GM crops is unfounded, as there is no evidence the GM crops have harmed human health or the environment. The only reason for organic farmers to fear contamination is rules that prevent foods from being certified as organic if they have even minute amounts of GM materials. If the anti-GM coalition wins this battle, it will be a loss for science and reason.

For over a decade, genetically modified [GM] crops have been one of the test issues for evidence-based policy. On the whole the US, unlike Europe, has been a haven of good sense. It has based policy on scientific evidence and has led the way in the development and cultivation of GM crops.

This is in stark contrast to most European countries, where such crops are banned or severely restricted and are regularly trashed by green vandals even when grown for research. But there are worrying signs that US policy is about to change.

Outside Europe, GM has been applied more rapidly and extensively than any other new technology in the history of farming. In 1996 GM crops covered some 1.7 million hectares worldwide. By 2009 the figure was 134 million hectares, much of it in the developing world. Various crops that will help reduce disease and hunger are nearing commercial cultivation, from golden rice that can prevent children going blind to crops that may help farmers in Africa cope with drought and avoid losses from pests and diseases.

GM cultivation has been most intensive in the US. Nearly all soya, cotton and corn in the country is now genetically modified, benefitting consumers, farmers and the environment. Herbicide-tolerant and pest-resistant crops have reduced the use of herbicides and pesticides, promoted no-till farming—so reducing soil erosion and carbon dioxide emissions—and have increased yields.

The world's leading science academies have all concluded that . . . there is no evidence that GM crops harm human health or the environment.

Contamination Rules

However, a coalition of anti-GM activists and a small but growing number of organic farmers are now making their influence felt in the US. In 2005, after field trials lasting eight years, the US Department of Agriculture (USDA) approved the cultivation of GM herbicide-tolerant alfalfa. The decision was challenged by activists, but after a lengthy review the USDA concluded that GM alfalfa should cause no concern for regulators, farmers or consumers. Nevertheless, under pressure from this coalition, the department is now considering strict rules on where the crops may be planted, to prevent "contamination" by GM seeds blown into fields of conventionally or organically grown alfalfa. A decision is expected this week.

The signs are not good. At a congressional hearing last Thursday [January 20, 2011], secretary for agriculture Tom Vilsack expressed his support for science-based policy and biotechnology, but ominously added that he supported the cultivation of organic products and would seek "co-existence" between GM and organic farmers. That implies restrictions on GM alfalfa to prevent contamination of organic fields. Farmers and companies that use and sell GM seeds and invest in research reasonably fear that if restrictions are imposed on GM alfalfa, limits on other GM crops will follow, and US policy will begin to converge with that of Europe.

Opposition to GM by green and organic lobbies is one of the main reasons why so many European Union countries ban or restrict their cultivation. It is a movement against science. The world's leading science academies have all concluded that, after 15 years of cultivation and consumption by millions of people, there is no evidence that GM crops harm human health or the environment.

Irrational rules deem that crops containing traces of genes from GM crops via cross-pollination cannot be certified as organic.

Organic Rules

By contrast the organic movement is based on the scientific fallacy that natural chemicals are good and synthetic chemicals bad. It ignores evidence and has consistently failed to substantiate any of its own claims. A meticulous review sponsored by the UK's [United Kingdom] Food Standards Agency recently found no evidence that organic food is more nutritious than conventionally grown food.

Meanwhile, irrational rules deem that crops containing traces of genes from GM crops via cross-pollination cannot be certified as organic. These rules can be, and have been, invoked to stop the cultivation of GM crops.

As for claims that organic farming is better for the environment, yields from organic farms are generally 20 to 50 per cent lower than those from conventional farms. Organic farming makes less efficient use of land while the world desperately needs the exact opposite.

Encouraged by the European Commission, which has confirmed scientific support for GM crops, attitudes in some EU [European Union] countries are changing. In the UK more friendly noises issue from the agricultural ministry, and the government's chief scientist, John Beddington, has stated that GM crops have a vital part to play in feeding the world. Meanwhile sales of organic food have declined. But if the US changes tack, green objectors will appear vindicated. Their influence in Europe will be enhanced and the consequences will be far-reaching. It will be a triumph for unreason.

10

Monsanto and Other Biotech Corporations Threaten World Food Production

Christopher D. Cook

Christopher D. Cook is a writer and the author of the 2006 book, Diet for a Dead Planet: Big Business and the Coming Food Crisis.

The world's food supply is threatened as large corporations such as Monsanto control more and more seeds with corporate patents. Genetically Modified [GM] seeds cannot be saved and reused by farmers or Monsanto will sue for patent infringement. GM crops may be causing an increase in food allergies, threaten to spread onto organic farms and into the environment, and some of the herbicide-resistant GM crops promote the use of more toxic herbicides. However, Europe, India, and even some pockets within the United States have banned the use of GM seeds, so corporate control of the food supply is not inevitable. The Barack Obama administration needs to reconsider its support for GM technology to bring it in line with international thinking and the needs of American food consumers.

Question: Would you want a small handful of government officials controlling America's entire food supply, all its seeds and harvests?

Christopher D. Cook, "Control Over Your Food: Why Monsanto's GM Seeds Are Undemocratic," *Christian Science Monitor*, February 23, 2011. www.csmonitor.com. Copyright © 2011 by Christopher D. Cook. All rights reserved. Reproduced by permission.

I suspect most would scream, "No way!"

Yet, while America seems allergic to public servants—with no profit motive in mind—controlling anything these days, a knee-jerk faith in the "free market" has led to overwhelming centralized control of nearly all our food stuffs, from farm to fork.

The [Barack] Obama administration's recent decision to radically expand genetically modified (GM) food—approving unrestricted production of agribusiness biotech company Monsanto's "Roundup Ready" alfalfa and sugar beets—marks a profound deepening of this centralization of food production in the hands of just a few corporations, with little but the profit motive to guide them.

Even as United States Department of Agriculture (USDA) officials enable a tighter corporate grip on the food chain, there is compelling evidence of GM foods' ecological and human health risks, suggesting we should at very least learn more before allowing their spread.

GM seeds . . . are non-replenishing and must be purchased anew each season, eliminating the time-honored farmer tradition of saving and re-using seeds.

Numerous peer-reviewed studies suggest these crops—the result of reformulating plant and animal genes, with minimal oversight and no food labeling disclosures—increase allergens in the food supply. And according to the World Health Organization, "The movement of genes from GM plants into conventional crops . . . may have an indirect effect on food safety and food security. This risk is real, as was shown when traces of a maize type which was only approved for feed use appeared in maize products for human consumption in the United States of America."

Corporate-Controlled Seeds Are Undemocratic

But these corporate-controlled seeds pose an even graver threat: Both the technology and economy of GM crops are intrinsically anti-democratic.

What's wrong with having a few corporations control virtually every aspect of our sustenance? Far from abstract, the genetic and proprietary control of our diets by a handful of companies (Monsanto, DuPont, and Syngenta combined own an astounding 47 percent of the global seed market) directly robs consumers and farmers of the most basic right to choose what they will eat and grow.

The entire concept of creating and selling patented GM seeds is based on proprietary corporate control: The seeds are non-replenishing and must be purchased anew each season, eliminating the time-honored farmer tradition of saving and re-using seeds.

Anyone doubting Monsanto's obsession with control can just ask just ask the thousands of farmers who have been sued and spied upon for alleged "seed piracy"—at least 2,391 farmers in 19 states through 2006, according to Monsanto website documents obtained by the Washington, DC-based Center for Food Safety (CFS). A report by CFS, using company records, found that "Monsanto has an annual budget of $10 million dollars and a staff of 75 devoted solely to investigating and prosecuting farmers."

Or ask Monsanto. Under the headline, "Why Does Monsanto Sue Farmers Who Save Seeds?" on its website, the firm states: "When farmers purchase a patented seed variety, they sign an agreement that they will not save and replant seeds produced from the seed they buy from us. More than 275,000 farmers a year buy seed under these agreements in the United States."

Threats to Food Safety and Biodiversity

The USDA, and even some leaders of the organics business such as Whole Foods and Stonyfield Farms, endorse the notion of "coexistence" between GM and organic crops—a comforting yet flawed claim. Numerous organic farmers have reported the unwanted arrival of GM seeds contaminating their fields, rendering organic crops unmarketable.

Even more troubling, "Roundup Ready" and other herbicide-resistant seeds by their nature promote the use of toxic herbicides—the use of which, contrary to industry claims, has risen as GM crops have proliferated, according to USDA data.

When our elected leaders . . . approve the expansion of risky seeds that endanger biodiversity as well as farmer and consumer choice, there should be more than a little outcry.

Even with buffer zones to segregate GM and organic fields, "Some degree of cross-pollination will occur regardless of what mechanism is going to be put in place," agronomist Jeff Wolt, of Iowa State University's Seed Science Center, told the *Associated Press.*

The GM threats to biodiversity and democracy are closely related. When you pair proprietary technology that's designed to retain company control of seeds (the very lifeblood of our food supply) along with highly concentrated market control, you get a hazardous blend of ecological, economic, and political centralization.

According to research of industry statistics by the nonprofit ETC (Action Group on Erosion, Technology and Concentration), "the top 3 seed companies control 65% of the proprietary maize seed market worldwide, and over half of the proprietary soybean seed market . . . Monsanto's biotech seeds and traits (including those licensed to other companies) accounted for 87% of the total world area devoted to genetically engineered seeds in 2007."

Of course, few of us think about market control when we're hustling through supermarket aisles getting our shopping done. But when our elected leaders (from both parties) approve the expansion of risky seeds that endanger biodiversity as well as farmer and consumer choice, there should be more than a little outcry.

Time and International Opinion Favor Biodiversity and Democracy

Genetically centralized control over seeds and the future of our food supply isn't inevitable. Over 80 towns across the state of Vermont, and numerous counties across the country have approved moratoria on GM crops. Monsanto has encountered mass farmer and political resistance in India and throughout much of Africa and Europe.

The Obama administration's effective rubber stamp on Monsanto's latest GM products is out of step with international thinking about food democracy and biodiversity, and an affront to that very American notion of consumer and producer choice—and voice—in the marketplace.

11

Biotech Company Monsanto Is Not a Threat to Food Production

Glen Brunkow

Glen Brunkow is a fifth-generation rancher and blogger from Kansas.

Criticism against the biotech company Monsanto, claiming that it is trying to corner the market on genetically modified (GM) seeds or that GM crops are bad for the environment and a danger to human health are unfounded. Monsanto's Round-up Ready products allow farmers to grow more food while employing farming methods that are better for the environment. As Monsanto developed the GM products, they have every right to market them for profit. Farmers can choose to buy these products or not. The complaints about Monsanto are based on the larger concern about modern farming practices. Farmers who want to go back to organic practices can do so, but those who want to use new technologies should be allowed to run their businesses the way they choose.

Let me throw this disclaimer out right off the bat. I do not work for Monsanto, I do not own stock in Monsanto and I really don't have any interest in Monsanto. Having said that I am writing this blog, as a farmer, in support of Monsanto.

Glenn Brunkow, "In Defense of Monsanto," *Dust on the Dashboard*, May 17, 2010. www.dustonthedashboard.blogspot.com. Copyright © 2010 by Glenn Brunkow. All rights reserved. Reproduced by permission.

Round-up Ready Benefits

Too often I see things written about the big, bad bully called Monsanto. Yes, they are the multi-national corporation that developed Round-up Ready soybeans and corn. For those of you not involved in agriculture, Round-up Ready soybeans and corn were a major technological breakthrough in agriculture. Monsanto developed a gene in corn and soybeans that allowed us to spray the chemical Round-up on those crops without killing them. Round-up is a herbicide that attacks green plant material. Yes, it is the same herbicide you spray on the cracks in your sidewalk.

This advancement allowed us to adopt environmentally friendly farming practices like no-till and has drastically reduced soil loss and fuel use on farms. It has also allowed us to use fewer herbicides on our crops. In short, Round-up technology allows us to grow more food, with less fertilizer, fewer chemicals and less fuel. All-the-while preserving our land in an environmentally friendly manner.

I applaud Monsanto and their innovation. They have allowed me to grow more food and save the environment.

Conspiracy Theories

Sounds great doesn't it. Well, there are many "environmental" groups that would muddy the waters and spread false information. They point toward Monsanto's patent on this technology and theorize that they are trying to monopolize the market on the very seed we use to grow your food. That is just not true. Yes, Monsanto is a for profit company and last time I checked this was the United States and we believed in the free market. Monsanto developed this technology and spent millions doing so, they have the right to make money. We farmers have the right not to buy their seed and I suspect in the near future we will have the right to buy the next, better innovation in farming technology. Do you think anyone will feel sorry for Monsanto?

As far as the idea they are cornering the market on seed. I want someone to prove it to me. No, I don't mean in shadowy Internet terms, I mean in real life, solid source terms. It's a conspiracy theory meant to cast doubt over modern farming practices.

Finally, the same shadowy, conspiracy theorists will claim that genetically modified organisms (GMOs) like Round-up Ready products will cause health problems in the future. First, what doesn't cause health problems and second, prove it. I have not seen one shred of credible evidence of any health risk from this technology.

So, I applaud Monsanto and their innovation. They have allowed me to grow more food and save the environment. If you want to go back to farming with heirloom vegetables and organic practices, then more power to you. It is a free country (for now) and we can all run our business as we see fit. Which is all I am really asking for. So if you don't mind I will continue to grow my Round-up Ready soybeans and corn and be a proud producer of the food we all eat.

12

Genetically Engineered Foods Should Be More Highly Regulated

Tom Philpott

Tom Philpott is the Cofounder of Maverick Farms, a center for sustainable food education in Valle Crucis, North Carolina, and a writer who focuses on food and agriculture topics.

The US Department of Agriculture (USDA) recently approved a new genetically modified (GM) type of Kentucky Bluegrass that will be able to withstand the Roundup herbicide. In doing so, the USDA dramatically reduced its already limited power to regulate GM crops. This is because the bluegrass approval admitted that the USDA has no authority to regulate GM crops as plant pests under the Plant Pest Act—historically the only regulatory method available for controlling GM crops. And if the USDA has no obligation to regulate GM crops, the courts have no way of intervening and the biotech industry can do whatever it wants with absolutely no oversight at all.

It's a hoary bureaucratic trick, making a controversial announcement on the Friday afternoon before a long weekend, when most people are daydreaming about what beer to buy on the way home from work, or are checking movie times online. But that's precisely what the US Department of Agriculture [USDA] pulled last Friday [July 1, 2011].

In an innocuous-sounding press release titled "USDA Responds to Regulation Requests Regarding Kentucky Bluegrass," agency officials announced their decision not to regulate a "Roundup Ready" strain of Kentucky bluegrass—that is, a strain genetically engineered to withstand glyphosate, Monsanto's widely used herbicide, which we know as Roundup. The maker of the novel grass seed, Scotts Miracle Gro, is now free to sell it far and wide. So you'll no doubt be seeing Roundup Ready bluegrass blanketing lawns and golf courses near you—and watching anal neighbors and grounds-keepers literally dousing the grass in weed killer without fear of harming a single precious blade.

Which is worrisome enough. But even more worrisome is the way this particular product was approved. According to Doug Gurian-Sherman, senior scientist at the Union of Concerned Scientists' Food and Environment Program, the documents released by the USDA's Animal and Plant Health Inspection Service (APHIS) along with the announcement portend a major change in how the feds will deal with genetically modified crops.

The USDA theoretically regulates new GMO crops the same way it would regulate, say, a backyard gardener's new crossbred squash variety. Which is to say, it really doesn't.

Weak Regulation of GMOs

Notably, given the already-lax regulatory regime governing GMOs (genetically modified organisms), APHIS seems to be *ramping down* oversight to the point where it is essentially meaningless. The new regime corresponding with the bluegrass announcement would "drastically weaken USDA's regulation," Gurian-Sherman told me. "This is perhaps the most serious change in US regs for [genetically modified] crops for many years."

Understanding why requires a brief history of the US government's twisted attempts to regulate GMOs. Since the Reagan days, federal regulatory efforts have been governed by what's known as the Coordinated Framework for Regulation of Biotechnology. Despite its name, the Coordinated Framework amounts to a porous hodgepodge of regulations based on the idea that overseeing GMOs required no new laws—that the novel technology could be effectively regulated under already-existing code.

Long story short, it means that the USDA theoretically regulates new GMO crops the same way it would regulate, say, a backyard gardener's new crossbred squash variety. Which is to say, it really doesn't. But that's absurd. GM crops pose different environmental threats than their nonmodified counterparts. The most famous example involves the rapid rise of Roundup Ready corn, soy, and cotton, which were introduced in the mid-late 1990s and now blanket tens of millions of acres of US farmland. Spraying all of that acreage every year with a single herbicide has given rise to a plague of Roundup-resistant "superweeds," forcing farmers to apply more and more Roundup and also resort to other, far-more-toxic products. Crops that aren't engineered to withstand an herbicide could never have created such a vexation.

The Fiction of the USDA's Regulation

From the start, in a tacit acknowledgement that modified crops really are different, the USDA has resorted to a fiction that allows it to at least nominally regulate GMOs, Gurian-Sherman told me. A '50s-era law called the Plant Pest Act gave the USDA power to restrict the introduction of organisms that might, well, harm plants. Genetically modified crops technically qualified as "plant pests" because industry scientists used DNA "promoters" derived from natural plant pathogens, most notably cauliflower mosaic virus, to amplify the genetic traits they introduced into new crops. "These promoters en-sure that the desired trait is always 'on,' that is, expressed," Gurian-Sherman explains.

The promoters—short stretches of DNA—are not them-selves expressed by the engineered plant. In other words, the cauliflower mosaic virus used to bolster, say, Roundup Ready soybeans, poses no threat to actual cauliflower plants. In addi-tion to promoters, GMO developers also use plant-pest sub-stances at other points in the genetic-modification process—but again, they don't express themselves in the finished project. "The Plant Pest Act was always just a regulatory hook to give the USDA authority to regulate engineered crops," notes Gurian-Sherman. "Everyone—the industry, industry watch-dogs, the USDA—always knew it was a fiction."

Yet the fiction has endured. The industry accepted it, Gurian-Sherman says, because cursory oversight gave compa-nies from a "fig leaf . . . They could say that their crops are regulated and have been deemed 'safe' by the USDA." GMO foes accepted it as well, he adds, because without the plant-pest fiction, the USDA would have *no* authority to regulate ge-netically modified crops. Indeed, this plant-pest business has given activists important tools to force better oversight. For instance, the USDA is required by the National Environmental Policy Act to assess the environmental impact of the novel crops it regulates, and by the Endangered Species Act to gauge potential impact of GM crops on endangered species. Well, in recent years, the Center for Food Safety has successfully sued the agency for failing to conduct proper environmental-impact statements and endangered-species analyses for crops it re-moved from its plant-pest list.

Then, in 2000, Congress passed the Plant Protection Act, which broadened the Plant Pest Act slightly, adding one more regulatory hook to the USDA's sparse GMO-regulation toolkit. That was the "noxious weed" status—any engineered crop that threatens to go rogue in the field and become a hard-to-control weed may be regulated.

That, roughly speaking, is where things stood. Until last Friday.

Obviously, a regulatory regime based on a lie was never really durable. Gurian-Sherman says the plant-pest schtick has been wearing thin for years now, because the industry has begun using nonpest material to develop novel crops. "If the companies don't use plant pests, then the USDA ostensibly doesn't have a legal hook to regulate the crops," he says. To compensate, Gurian-Sherman says, the agency has resorted to tacitly acknowledging that it has no jurisdiction, but doing so quietly to avoid exposing the fiction.

USDA's Admission That It Lacks Jurisdiction

But the agency's decision on Scotts Miracle Gro's Roundup Ready bluegrass may have changed all that. Scotts essentially shattered the code of silence in a Sept. 13, 2010 letter to the USDA, which the agency released Friday. The company declared:

> Because Kentucky bluegrass itself is not a plant pest, no plant pest components will be involved in the transformation, and the native plant genomes that will be used are fully classified, there is no scientifically valid basis for concluding that transgenic Kentucky bluegrass is or will become a plant pest within the meaning of the Plant Protection Act.

Based on that impeccable logic, the company went in the for the kill: "Scotts requests that [USDA] confirm that Kentucky bluegrass modified without plant pest components . . . is not a regulated article within the meaning of the current regulations."

In its July 1 response, the USDA agreed: "[N]one of the organisms used in generating this genetically engineered (GE) glyophosphate tolerant Kentucky bluegrass . . . are considered to be plant pests," so Roundup Ready bluegrass "does not meet the definition of a 'regulated article' and is not subject" to the Plant Protection Act. In other words, go forth and multiply.

On Friday, the agency also retracted its only other hook for regulating GM crops—the noxious-weeds provision. The Center for Food Safety had petitioned the USDA to classify genetically modified bluegrass as a noxious weed. The case for this is strong: Gurian-Sherman explains that bluegrass has light pollen that can be carried for miles on the wind, meaning that genetically modified bluegrass can easily transfer its genes to established conventional bluegrass.

And like most grasses, bluegrass spreads rapidly. Anyone who has ever grown a garden can testify that it's tough to get rid of unwanted turf grass. In fact, Scotts is also seeking deregulation of Roundup Ready bentgrass, another grass that has proven hard to control. In 2005, Scotts grew trial plots of its bentgrass in Oregon. It escaped the boundaries of the experimental plot and is *still* creating problems for homeowners miles away.

If the USDA doesn't regulate novel GMOs, then it has no obligation to perform environmental-impact or endangered-species analyses of new organisms in the biotech pipeline.

In one of the document released last Friday, the USDA conceded that, by its own reckoning, Scotts' genetically modified bluegrass "can be considered for regulation as a Federally listed noxious weed that shows potential to cause damage to crops and natural resources of the United States." But to avoid actually declaring it a noxious weed, the agency simply claimed that the weed risks posed by genetically engineered and conventional are "essentially the same."

That's highly debatable, since anyone who wants to address weed problems from conventional bluegrass can turn to

Roundup, the nation's most-used herbicide, whereas dealing with rogue Roundup Ready bluegrass means resorting to chemicals far more toxic. Starting with the "essentially the same" premise, the USDA notes that conventional bluegrass is already widely planted across the country without causing much harm; from there it assumes that Scotts' engineered bluegrass won't be a problem either, concluding that it need not be declared a "noxious weed" after all. And if it's neither a plant pest nor a noxious weed, the USDA has no right or obligation to regulate it. Game, set, match to Scotts Miracle Gro. Or, to use a more appropriate sports metaphor: a hole in one for Scotts!

Free Rein for the Biotech Industry

So where does this leave us? If the plant-pest fiction no longer applies, and if even crops that carry an obvious noxious-weed risk won't be regulated as such, then what happens?

Well, if the USDA doesn't regulate novel GMOs, then it has no obligation to perform environmental-impact or endangered-species analyses of new organisms in the biotech pipeline, including plants engineered as pharmaceutical substances and biofuel feedstocks. In an email exchange, a USDA press officer confirmed that the agency would not be conducting an environmental-impact statement on Roundup Ready bluegrass—and by extension, any other crops that don't count as plant pests or noxious weeds.

The [biotech] industry gets free rein to plant whatever it wants—wherever it wants.

And that means watchdogs like Center for Food Safety will no longer have a legal foothold to sue the USDA for regulating those things badly—which is usually how it's done. In the wake of several recent deregulations—including Roundup Ready sugar beets, alfalfa, and bentgrass—federal courts have sided with Center for Food Safety and rebuked the USDA for failing to properly assess risks. Are such lawsuits, essentially the last line of defense for GMO regulation, a thing of the past? "We're still analyzing the documents," says George Kimbrell, the center's senior attorney.

But Kimbrell made an important point: "Look, [the USDA] is a rogue agency," he said. "It has been rebuked time and time again by the courts for its failed oversight of these crops."

Implication: Take away the plant-pest and noxious-weed hooks and the courts can no longer intervene. The industry gets free rein to plant whatever it wants—wherever it wants. This development worries Gurian-Sherman. "Will some companies still want to have the fig leaf of USDA regulation even if they're not using plant-pest material? Probably," he says. "But they don't have to. It's now their choice."

Moreover, he adds, "the noxious-weed standard has been set so high as to be virtually meaningless." The message to industry is clear: "You can completely skirt the regulatory process."

13

Genetically Engineered Foods Should Be Less Regulated

Dick Taverne

Dick Taverne is the founder of Sense About Science, an independent charitable trust based in London that promotes a science-based approach to genetically engineered foods and other public issues.

Scientific testing over 15 years has shown that genetically modified (GM) foods are not a threat to human health or the environment, yet excessive regulation and testing requirements in both the United States and Britain have kept GM technology from saving millions of lives in the developing world. Unlike other types of crops modified by less precise methods of gene modification, GM crops face unfair regulatory obstacles that hamper development. The main reason for GM overregulation is a misinformed public's outcry that GM foods are a health threat or pose an environmetal hazard. GM crops will eventually be accepted around the world but the delays caused by anti-GM advocates have been very costly.

GM [genetically modified] foods are safe, healthy and essential if we ever want to achieve decent living standards for the world's growing population. Misplaced moralising about them in the west is costing millions of lives in poor countries.

The Dream of Golden Rice and Other GM Crops

Seven years ago, *Time* magazine featured the Swiss biologist Ingo Potrykus on its cover. As the principal creator of genetically modified rice—or "golden rice"—he was hailed as potentially one of mankind's great benefactors. Golden rice was to be the start of a new green revolution to improve the lives of millions of the poorest people in the world. It would help remedy vitamin A deficiency, the cause of 1–2m [million] deaths a year, and could save up to 500,000 children a year from going blind. It was the flagship of plant biotechnology. No other scientific development in agriculture in recent times held out greater promise.

Seven years later, the most optimistic forecast is that it will take another five or six years before golden rice is grown commercially. The realisation of Potrykus's dream keeps receding. The promised benefits from other GM crops that should reduce hunger and disease have been equally elusive. GM crops should now be growing in areas where no crops can grow: drought-resistant crops in arid soil and salt-resistant crops in soil of high salinity. Plant-based oral vaccines should now be saving millions of deaths from diarrhoea and hepatitis B; they can be ingested in orange juice, bananas or tomatoes, avoiding the need for injection and for trained staff to administer them and refrigeration to store them.

None of these crops is yet on the market. What has gone wrong? Were the promises unrealistic, or is GM technology, as its opponents claim, flawed—because of possible harm to human safety or the environment or because it is ill-suited to the needs of poor farmers in the developing world.

Suspicions About GM Food

Public discussion of GM food in the British media, and throughout Europe, reflects a persistent suspicion of GM crops. Supermarkets display notices that their products are

"GM-free." Sales of organic food, promoted as a natural alternative to the products of modern scientific farming, are increasing by about 20 per cent a year. Indeed, EU [European Union] regulations, based on the precautionary principle, provide safeguards against "contamination" of organic farms by GM crops; they require any produce containing more than 0.9 per cent GM content to be labelled as such, with the clear implication that it needs a health warning and should be avoided. This causes a major conflict over GM soya beans imported from America. Some GM crops are taking root in some European countries, but in most they are in effect banned. The public is led to believe that GM technology is not only unsafe but harmful to the environment, and that it only serves to profit big agricultural companies.

GM food crops for the developing world [have] been delayed ... because GM crops, unlike conventional crops, must overcome costly, time-consuming and unnecessary regulatory obstacles.

Seldom has public perception been more out of line with the facts. The public in Britain and Europe seems unaware of the astonishing success of GM crops in the rest of the world. No new agricultural technology in recent times has spread faster and more widely. Only a decade after their commercial introduction, GM crops are now cultivated in 22 countries on over 100m hectares (an area more than four times the size of Britain) by over 10m farmers, of whom 9m are resource-poor farmers in developing countries, mainly India and China. Most of these small-scale farmers grow pest-resistant GM cotton. In India alone, production tripled last year to over 3.6m hectares. This cotton benefits farmers because it reduces the need for insecticides, thereby increasing their income and also improving their health. It is true that the promised development of staple GM food crops for the developing world has been delayed, but this is not because of technical flaws. It is principally because GM crops, unlike conventional crops, must overcome costly, time-consuming and unnecessary regulatory obstacles before they can be licensed.

The nature of GM technology makes it unlikely that it is more dangerous than conventional farming.

No Evidence of Harm to Human or the Environment

The alleged risk to health from GM crops is still the main reason for public disquiet—something nurtured by statements by environmental NGO[Non-governmental organization]s, who in 2002 even persuaded the Zambian government to reject food aid from the US at a time of famine because some of it was derived from GM crops. This allegation of harm has been so soundly and frequently refuted that when it is repeated, the temptation is to despair. But unless the charge is confronted, contradicted and disproved whenever it is made, its credibility will persist.

The fact is that there is not a shred of any evidence of risk to human health from GM crops. Every academy of science, representing the views of the world's leading experts—the Indian, Chinese, Mexican, Brazilian, French and American academies as well as the Royal Society, which has published four separate reports on the issue—has confirmed this. Independent inquiries have found that the risk from GM crops is no greater than that from conventionally grown crops that do not have to undergo such testing. In 2001, the research directorate of the EU commission released a summary of 81 scientific studies financed by the EU itself—not by private industry— conducted over a 15-year period, to determine whether GM products were unsafe or insufficiently tested: none found evidence of harm to humans or to the environment.

No Dangers in GM Technology

Indeed, the nature of GM technology makes it unlikely that it is more dangerous than conventional farming. Throughout history, farmers have sought to improve their crops by cross-breeding plants with desirable characteristics. Cross-breeding, however, is a lottery and its consequences cannot be easily predicted. Small genetic changes that are desirable may be accompanied by others that are undesirable. It may take generations of back-crossing to eliminate unwanted characteristics. The process is therefore not only unpredictable but slow and expensive, and may even be risky.

One of the most effective standard methods of breeding to obtain improved crops is to bombard seeds and plants with gamma rays to alter their DNA by causing mutations, some of which can then be selected for a desired trait. (Incidentally, organic farmers, in their desire to avoid artificial chemicals, are even more dependent than conventional farmers on crop varieties generated by irradiation.) Irradiation alters both chromosome structure and genome sequence in a way that is quite random. Moreover, there is no legal requirement to test such irradiated products either for effects on health or for what they might do to the environment.

Worldwide experience of GM crops to date provides strong evidence that they actually benefit the environment.

By contrast, genetic modification in the laboratory introduces a well-characterised gene or genes into an established genetic background without big disruption. What such modification does is what plant breeding has always done, but more quickly and accurately. Opponents often argue that GM technology is different because it can transfer genes between species. But again, this is nothing new, as during evolutionary time genes have moved between species naturally. That is why we have such a diversity of plant life.

Also, those who oppose genetic modification in agriculture often embrace the technology in medicine. The human insulin used to treat diabetes, for example, is genetically engineered: the human gene that codes for insulin has been transferred into bacteria and yeast, a process that involves crossing the species barrier. By what rationale can the technology be safe and ethical when saving lives in medical treatment, but not when used to make plants resistant to pests in order to save people from hunger?

Environmental Concerns Unfounded

Some opponents of GM crops, who seem to have realised that the argument based on lack of safety has no basis, now focus their opposition on environmental concerns, arguing that GM crops destroy biodiversity. It would be wrong to claim that the planting of GM crops could never have adverse environmental effects. But their impact depends on circumstances, on the particular crop and environment in which it is grown. Such effects occur with all sorts of agriculture. Worldwide experience of GM crops to date provides strong evidence that they actually benefit the environment. They reduce reliance on agrochemical sprays, save energy, use less fossil fuels in their production and reduce the emissions of greenhouse gases. And by improving yields, they make better use of scarce agricultural land.

These findings were reported by Graham Brookes and Peter Barfoot of PG Economics in a careful study of the global effects of GM crops in their first ten years of commercial use, from 1996 to 2005. They concluded that the "environmental impact" of pesticide and herbicide use in GM-growing countries had been reduced by 15 per cent and 20 per cent respectively. Energy-intensive cultivation is being replaced by no-till or low-till agriculture. More than a third of the soya bean crop grown in the US is now grown in unploughed fields. Apart from using less energy, avoiding the plough has many environmental advantages. It improves soil quality, causes less disturbance to life within it and diminishes the emission of methane and other greenhouse gases. The study concluded that "the carbon savings from reduced fuel use and soil carbon sequestration in 2005 were equal to removing 4m cars from the road (equal to 17 per cent of all registered cars in the UK)."

One other effect of GM crops may be the most significant of all. In the next half century, the world will have to more than double its food production to feed the over 800m people who now go hungry, the extra 3bn [billion] expected by 2050 and the hundreds of millions of people who will, as living standards rise, acquire a more western lifestyle and eat a great deal more meat. At the same time, the world is running out of good farming land and water resources. Shortage of land already causes subsistence farmers in Indonesia and South America to slash and burn tropical forests. More droughts and desertification caused by global warming will make matters worse. So will the manufacture of biofuels from wheat, corn and other food crops that further diminishes the supply of land for growing food and thus pushes up prices. Improved yields from GM technology lead to better use of land and prevent the destruction of forests with its effect on global warming. By contrast, the environmentalist James Lovelock has estimated that if all farming became organic, we would only be able to feed one third of even the present world population.

Burdensome Regulation of GM Crops

Given the evidence about the safety of GM crops and their beneficial environmental impact, and given the global success of GM cotton, maize and soya, why have so few staple GM food crops been licensed for commercial growth? Why are the benefits of golden rice, drought or salt-resistant crops, plant-based vaccines and other GM products with special promise for the developing world so long delayed?

***

The story of Potrykus's golden rice suggests one explanation. The development of the product itself was a great scientific achievement. A bacterial gene together with two genes from the daffodil were inserted into rice to make it synthesise the micronutrient "β-carotene," which when eaten is converted into vitamin A. This process took ten years. Many more years were spent, with the help of Syngenta and other biotech companies, in solving the patent problems to enable golden rice to be made available to small-scale farmers without royalty payments. Then began the struggle to obtain regulatory approval.

First, although it is agreed even by those opposed to the technology that the presence of β-carotene in the rice grain presents no possible risk to the environment, no experimental small-scale field trials are permitted. So all rice plants must be grown in specific plant growth chambers in greenhouses—processes that take three years. Each plant must be shown to be the product of one gene transfer into the same part of its DNA. Then its proteins must be extracted and fractionated, characterised biochemically and their function confirmed—analyses that take at least two years of intensive work in a well-equipped laboratory. Next, feeding experiments in rodents are required, though most people have happily eaten these genes and the proteins they code for from other sources throughout their lives and though the proteins produced from the daffodil genes bear no relation to any toxin or allergen. No slight hypothetical risk may be left untested.

It is ironic that other varieties of rice grown all over southeast Asia have been shown to be "genetically modified" too, but accidentally as the result of mutations, chromosomal recombinations, translocations of pieces of DNA and even deletions of sections of DNA. This rice is consumed everywhere without the requirement of any laboratory tests.

The scientific way of ensuring that crops are safe is to test the product, not the process. Perversely, regulations in the US as well as Europe require the opposite. The result is that it takes much longer and costs at least ten times as much to bring a new GM crop to market as an equivalent conventionally bred crop. As Potrykus has pointed out, no scientist or scientific institution in the public domain has the funding or the motivation to go through such an expensive and drawn-out procedure. Only large companies or the most richly funded charities can and the only projects companies are likely to back are those that make big profits. Producing rice that saves the lives or the eyesight of millions of the poorest peasants offers no great financial rewards.

The broader driving force behind the excessive regulation of GM crops . . . is the cult of "back to nature," which has also inspired the propaganda against agricultural biotechnology.

Why is a technology which has so much to contribute impeded by regulations that make no sense? Part of the blame lies with the large agrobusinesses. They initially welcomed elaborate regulation to discourage competition from small companies that could not afford the cost. Indeed, they successfully resisted every attempt by advisers in the [Ronald] Reagan administration to regulate each GM crop simply as a new product, rather than by the process by which it was derived, an approach that would have treated GM and conventionally grown crops similarly and made more scientific sense. But the large companies won, and the concentration of agricultural biotechnology in the hands of a few giants, like Monsanto, is the result. Furthermore, although tight regulation was backed by some supporters of GM who believed it would reassure the public, it has had the opposite effect. If governments appear to think it necessary to take extreme precautions, the public will conclude that the technology must be dangerous. A third element has been mistrust of multinationals. This has intensified opposition to GM crops because it is widely felt that companies are the main, if not the only, beneficiaries—and that, since they are responsible for most of the development of the crops, this must be subject to the strictest possible regulation. The inept PR [public relations] that accompanied Monsanto's introduction of GM crops to Europe was also bitterly criticised by other agrobusinesses.

The Back to Nature Cult

The broader driving force behind the excessive regulation of GM crops, however, is the cult of "back to nature," which has also inspired the propaganda against agricultural biotechnology as a whole. This cult has many manifestations. One is the popularity of organic farming, which is based on the manifestly false principle that artificial chemicals are bad and natural chemicals good. Another is the rising fashion for alternative, non-evidence based medicine. The dogmatic opponents of GM crops in Europe believe that interference with the genetic make-up of plants is essentially a moral issue. It is to be condemned as part of mankind's sinful attempt to control nature, which contributes to global warming, to epidemics of cancer and all the blights of modern life. . . .

There can be little doubt that GM crops will be accepted worldwide in time, even in Europe. But in delaying cultivation, the anti-GM lobbies have exacted a heavy price. Their opposition has undermined agrobusiness in Europe and has driven abroad much research into plant biotechnology—an area in which Britain formerly excelled. Over-regulation may well cause the costs of the technology to remain higher than they need be. Above all, delay has caused the needless loss of millions of lives in the developing world. These lobbies and their friends in the organic movement have much to answer for.

Organizations to Contact

The editors have compiled the following list of organizations concerned with the issues debated in this book. The descriptions are derived from materials provided by the organizations. All have publications or information available for interested readers. The list was compiled on the date of publication of the present volume; names; addresses, phone and fax numbers, and e-mail and Internet addresses may change. Be aware that many organizations take several weeks or longer to respond to inquiries, so allow as much time as possible.

Center for Food Safety (CFS)
660 Pennsylvania Ave. SE, #302, Washington, DC   20003
(202) 547-9359 • fax: (202) 547-9429
e-mail: office@centerforfoodsafety.org
website: www.centerforfoodsafety.org

The Center for Food Safety (CFS) was founded by the International Center for Technology Assessment in 1997 to assess new technologies being used for food production and to offer alternative methods that provide sustainable food sources. CFS opposes the commercial release of genetically engineered food products without rigorous testing to ensure their safety, contends that all genetically engineered foods should be labeled, and believes that cloned animals and genetically engineered fish should not be used in food production. The organization provides educational materials to the public and the media, and suggests guidelines to policymakers. Publications and reports, including, "Genetically Modified (GM) Crops and Foods: Worldwide Regulation, Prohibition and Production," can be found on the CFS website.

Council for Responsible Genetics (CRG)
5 Upland Rd., Suite 3, Cambridge, MA   02140
(617) 868-0870 • fax: (617) 491-5344
e-mail: crg@gene-watch.org
website: www.gene-watch.org

The Council for Responsible Genetics (CRG) works to provide accurate and current information about emerging biotechnologies so that citizens can play a more active role in shaping policies regarding these advances. Specific topics addressed by the organization include genetic determinism, cloning and human genetic manipulation, and constructing and promoting a "Genetic Bill of Rights." *Gene Watch* is the bimonthly publication of CRG; articles from this magazine as well as other institute reports are accessible on the CRG website.

Greenpeace
702 H St. NW, Suite 300, Washington, DC   20001
(202) 462-1177 • fax: (202) 462-4507
e-mail: info@wdc.greenpeace.org
website: www.greenpeace.org

Greenpeace is an activist group seeking to protect the environment worldwide. Current focuses of the organization include combating global warming, deforestation, and ocean pollution. Additionally, Greenpeace opposes the genetic engineering of food and food sources, and contends that any genetically engineered food on the market should be labeled. Reports on the threat of genetic engineering to the environment, as well as reports on other topics can be downloaded from the Greenpeace website.

Institute for Responsible Technology (IRT)
PO Box 469, Fairfield, IA   52556
(641) 209-1765
e-mail: info@responsibletechnology.org
website: www.responsibletechnology.org

The Institute for Responsible Technology (IRT) is an organization founded by author Jeffrey Smith to educate policy makers and the public about genetically modified (GM) foods and crops. IRT investigates and reports on the risks of GM crops and their impact on health, environment, the economy, and agriculture, as well as the problems associated with current research, regulation, corporate practices, and reporting. The IRT website is a source of online videos, podcasts, blogs, and reports on this topic. Publications include *The Non-GMO Shopping Guide* and *State-of-the-Science on the Health Risks of GM Foods.*

International Bioethics Committee (IBC)
2 United Nations Plaza, Room 900, New York, NY   10017
(212) 963-5995 • fax: (212) 963-8014
e-mail: ibc@unesco.org
website: www.unesco.org/ibc

The International Bioethics Committee (IBC) is a committee within the United Nations Educational, Scientific, and Cultural Organization (UNESCO). The 36 independent experts that make up the committee meet to ensure that human dignity and freedom are observed and respected in biotechnological advances worldwide. The biotechnology programme at UNESCO seeks to strengthen research in this field in the hopes of aiding national development and worldwide socioeconomic growth. The IBC has authored declarations such as the *Universal Declaration on Bioethics and Human Rights* to provide guidelines for those working in the fields of biotechnology. These declarations, as well as publications including reports, policy briefs, a periodical called *A World of Science,* and newsletters can be viewed online.

Monsanto Company
800 N. Lindbergh Blvd., St. Louis, MO   63167
(314) 694-1000
website: www.monsanto.com

The Monsanto Company is a US-based multinational agricultural biotechnology corporation. It is the world's leading producer of the herbicide glyphosate, marketed as "Roundup," and one of the largest producers of genetically modified (GM) seeds and crops. Under the News & Views section of the company's website, there is a topic entitled Issues & Answers that provides Monsanto's positions on various hot issues being debated about GM crops, including "Saved Seed & Farmer Lawsuits," "Biotech/GMO Safety & Advantages," and "Monsanto's Business Practices."

Nuffield Council on Bioethics

Communications & External Affairs Manager
London   WC1B 3JS
(020) 7681 9619
e-mail: bioethics@nuffieldbioethics.org
website: www.nuffieldbioethics.org

Established in 1991, the Nuffield Council on Bioethics works to identify and address ethical issues connected with current and emerging biotechnologies. The council also provides educational information to the public to stimulate discussion and debate about these technologies. The Nuffield Council's website offers copies of papers it has published, including *Genetically Modified Crops: Ethical and Social Issues.*

Pew Charitable Trust

901 E St. NW, Washington, DC   20004-2008
(202) 552-2000 • fax: (202) 552-2299
e-mail: info@pewtrusts.org
website: www.pewtrusts.org

The Pew Charitable Trusts is an independent nonprofit organization funded by seven individual charitable funds established by the children of Sun Oil Company founder Joseph N. Pew and his wife, Mary Anderson Pew. The group conducts research on public policy issues in partnership with donors, public and private organizations, and concerned citizens, with the goal of finding fact-based solutions and investments to improve society. Although it concluded its work in 2007, the Pew Initiative on Food and Biotechnology collected research and spotlighted policy issues on the topic of agricultural biotechnology, and its resource materials are still available on its website. Publications include, *Lessons Learned: Food for Thought and Discussion* and *US vs. EU: An Examination of the Trade Issues Surrounding Genetically Modified Food.*

Sierra Club

85 Second St., 2nd Floor, San Francisco, CA   94105

(415) 977-5500 • fax: (415) 977-5797

e-mail: information@sierraclub.org

website: www.sierraclub.org

Founded in 1892, the Sierra Club works to ensure that the planet is protected and preserved. With regards to genetically engineered organisms (GEOs), Sierra Club maintains that a moratorium on the planting and release of any GEOs should be observed until extensive testing has been done to ensure their safety for both humans and the environment. The organization also opposes the patenting of GEOs and the genetic code of humans. *Sierra* is the bimonthly magazine of the Sierra Club; articles from this publication and others specific to the issue of genetic engineering are available online. A search of the website produces publications such as *The Risks of GE Foods* as well as additional information on genetic engineering.

Union of Concerned Scientists (UCS)

2 Brattle Square, Cambridge, MA   02138-3780

(617) 547-5552 • fax: (617) 864-9405

website: www.ucsusa.org

UCS is a membership organization of citizens and scientists who work together to promote the responsible use of science to improve the world. UCS has extensively researched and reported on the use of genetic engineering (GE) in food and plant products, as well as on the cloning of animals in the food production chain, generally advocating a precautionary approach to the use of these products. The organization argues that more testing must be conducted before GE crops and animals for food production can be considered safe and suitable for inclusion in the marketplace. The UCS website contains a section on Food & Agriculture, which examines the impacts of genetic engineering and provides additional reports and factsheets, including *Failure to Yield: Evaluating the*

Performance of Genetically Engineered Crops and *No Sure Fix: Prospects for Reducing Nitrogen Fertilizer Pollution through Genetic Engineering.*

US Food and Drug Administration (FDA)

10903 New Hampshire Ave., Silver Spring, MD   20993-0002
(888) 463-6332
website: www.fda.gov

The FDA is the US government agency responsible for ensuring the quality and safety of all food and drug products sold in the United States. As such, the FDA has conducted extensive tests to evaluate the safety of genetically engineered (GE) foods and has issued guidelines and regulatory measures to control what types of GE products make it to market. The Center for Veterinary Medicine (CVM), an office within the FDA, specifically examines the impact of GE products on animals and has also researched and reported on the cloned animals that will be used in the food industry. Reports by both the FDA and CVM can be retrieved from the FDA website.

Bibliography

Books

Geoffrey S. Becker and Tadlock Cowan — *Biotechnology in Animal Agriculture: Status and Current Issues*, Charleston, SC: BiblioGov, 2010.

Luc Bodiguel and Michael Cardwell — *The Regulation of Genetically Modified Organisms: Comparative Approaches*, New York: Oxford University Press, 2010.

Conrad G. Brunk and Harold Coward — *Acceptable Genes?: Religious Traditions and Genetically Modified Foods*, Albany, NY: State University of New York Press, 2009.

Colin Carter, GianCarlo Moschini and Ian Sheldon — *Genetically Modified Food and Global Welfare*, Bingley, United Kingdom: Emerald Group Publishing Limited, 2011.

Jeri Freedman — *Genetically Modified Food: How Biotechnology Is Changing What We Eat*, New York: Rosen Publishing Group, 2009.

Lindsay M. Grover — *Genetically Engineered Crops: Biotechnology, Biosafety and Benefits*, Hauppauge, NY: Nova Science Publishing Inc., 2011.

Miriam Jumba — *Genetically Modified Organisms: The Mystery Unraveled*, Bloomington, IN: Trafford Publishing, 2010.

Richard E. Just, Julian M. Alston and David Zilberman — *Regulating Agricultural Biotechnology: Economics and Policy*, New York: Springer, 2006.

Gary E. Marchant, Guy A. Cardineau and Thomas P. Redick, eds. — *Thwarting Consumer Choice: The Case Against Mandatory Labeling for Genetically Modified Foods*, Staten Island, NY: Aei Press, R&L, 2010.

Beiquan Mou and Ralph Scorza, eds. — *Transgenic Horticultural Crops: Challenges and Opportunities*, Oxford, United Kingdom: Taylor & Francis, 2011.

Marion Nestle — *Safe Food: The Politics of Food Safety*, Berkely, CA: University of California Press, 2003.

Robert Paarlberg — *Starved for Science: How Biotechnology Is Being Kept Out of Africa*, Cambridge, MA: Harvard University Press, 2009.

Mark A. Pollack and Gregory C. Shaffer — *When Cooperation Fails: The International Law and Politics of Genetically Modified Foods*, New York: Oxford University Press, 2009.

Pamela C. Ronald and R. W. Adamchak — *Tomorrow's Table: Organic Farming, Genetics, and the Future of Food*, New York: Oxford University Press, 2008.

Katelin Schug — *Introduction To Genetically Modified Foods—WARNING: You Could Be Eating Dangerous Food!* Amazon Digital Services, 2011.

Rachel Schurman and William A. Munro — *Fighting for the Future of Food: Activists versus Agribusiness in the Struggle over Biotechnology*, Minneapolis: University of Minnesota Press, 2010.

Robert Smithdeal — *How To Eat with Confidence And Peace of Mind by Easily Identifying And Avoiding Genetically Modified Foods*, Amazon Digital Services, 2011.

Linda Tagliaferro — *Genetic Engineering: Modern Progress or Future Peril?*, Minneapolis, MN: Twenty-First Century Books, 2009.

Paul B. Thompson, ed. — *Food Biotechnology in Ethical Perspective*, New York: Springer, 2007.

Lisa H. Weasel — *Food Fray: Inside the Controversy over Genetically Modified Food*, New York: AMACOM, 2008.

Periodicals and Internet Sources

Rady Ananda — "After 20 Years, Nearly Everyone Still Wants GM Food to Be Labeled," thepeoplesvoice.org, March 5, 2011. www.thepeoplesvoice.org.

Alisa Baumer — "Labels for Genetically Modified Foods," FoodEditorials.com, accessed September 13, 2011. www.street directory.com.

Mark Bittman — "Profits Before Environment," *New York Times*, August 30, 2011. http://opinionator.blogs.nytimes.com.

Mark Bittman — "Why Aren't G.M.O. Foods Labeled?," *New York Times*, February 15, 2011. http://opinionator.blogs.nytimes.com.

Brendan Borrell — "Food Fight: The Case for Genetically Modified Food," *Scientific American*, April 11, 2011. www.scientificamerican.com.

Terra Brockman — "Fooling the World, Not Feeding It," *Zester Daily*, June 16, 2010. www.zesterdaily.com.

Susan Carpenter — "Genetically Engineered Salmon Must Be Labeled, California Assembly Bill Says," *Los Angeles Times*, May 6, 2011. http://latimes blogs.latimes.com.

The Economist — "The Adoption of Genetically Modified Crops: Growth Areas," February 23, 2011. www.economist.com.

Monica Eng — "With No Labeling, Few Realize they Are Eating Genetically Modified Foods," *Chicago Tribune*, May 24, 2011.

Barry Estabrook — "Genetically Modified Alfalfa Officially on the Way," *The Atlantic*, January 28, 2011.

Nina V. Fedoroff — "Engineering Food for All," *New York Times*, August 18, 2011.

Carey Gillam — "U.S. Organic Food Industry Fears GMO Contamination," *Reuters*, March 12, 2008.

Paul Greenberg — "An Engineered Salmon's Fishy Agenda: How a Corporate-Created Fish Won't Solve Any Problems, But May Create Some," *Salon*, June 2, 2011. www.salon.com.

Richard Hines and Clare Oxborrow — "Who Benefits from GM Crops?—The Rise in Pesticide Use," *Pesticides News*, Issue 79, March 2008. www.pan-uk.org.

Mary Clare Jalonick — "GM Food Is Hard For Shoppers To Avoid," *The Huffington Post*, February 25, 2011. www.huffingtonpost.com.

Robert Langreth and Matthew Herper — "The Planet Versus Monsanto," *Forbes*, December 31, 2009.

Joseph Mercola — "19 Studies Link GMO Foods to Organ Disruption," Mercola.com, April 27, 2011. http://articles .mercola.com.

Rosie Mestel — "GMO Food Labeling Fight," *Los Angeles Times*, April 20, 2010. http://latimesblogs.latimes.com.

Brad Newsome — "Gene Genius Is the Future of Food," *Sydney Morning Herald*, April 28, 2011. www.smh.com.au.

Tom Philpott — "Attack of the Monsanto Super-insects," *Mother Jones*, August 30, 2011.

Elizabeth Rosen — "Rejecting Genetically Modified Foods," *Cornell Daily Sun*, February 15, 2011. http://cornellsun.com.

ScienceDaily   "U.S. Government Urged to Rule on Consumption of Genetically Engineered Salmon," August 5, 2011. www.sciencedaily.com.

Slow Food USA "The Slow Food USA Blog: Organic Farmers v Monsanto," June 10, 2011. www.slowfoodusa.org.

Jeffrey Smith   "10 Reasons to Avoid GMOs," *Institute for Responsible Technology*, August 25, 2011. www.responsible technology.org.

Union of Concerned Scientists "FEED: Genetically Engineered Sweet Corn, Coming to a Market Near You," September 2011. www.ucs usa.org.

Index

A

Action Group on Erosion, Technology and Concentration (ETC), 66–67
Africa, 60, 67
Agrobusiness. *See* Biotechnology companies
Agrochemicals. *See* Herbicides; Pesticides
Alfalfa, 10, 55, 60–61, 64
Allergens
  are increased by GE foods, 8, 15, 16, 32
  pollen, 38
  soybeans with Brazil nut genes, 16, 32
  StarLink corn, 16, 57
Animal and Plant Health Inspection Service (APHIS), 72
Animal feed contamination, 10
Antibiotic resistance marker genes (ARM), 12, 17, 32, 37–38
Antibiotics
  increased use in cows, 15–16
  resistance, 17, 32, 37–38
Antioxidants, 31
Antoniou, Michael, 13
APHIS (Animal and Plant Health Inspection Service), 72
AquaBounty Technologies. *See* Salmon
AquAdvantage salmon. *See* Salmon
ARM genes, 12, 17, 32, 37–38
Astra-Zeneca. *See* Syngenta
Atrazine, 51
Atriplex, 46

Austria, 8
Aventis, 11, 18
  See also Biotechnology companies
Axelrod, David, 55

B

Bacillus thuringiensis, 9, 34
  See also Bt corn
Bacteria
  antibiotic resistance, 17, 32, 37–38
  Bacillus thuringiensis, 9, 34
  L-tryptophan contamination, 14, 32
  rBGH milk, 17
  soil contamination, 19
  vectors, markers and promoters, 12, 13, 14, 86
Bans
  ARM genes, 17
  Canada, 16
  corn, 8
  Europe, 7, 8, 16, 27, 61, 81
  global, 67
  rBGH, 16
  seeds, 7
  soybeans, 81
  Venezuela, 8
  Vermont, 67
  See also Regulations
Barfoot, Peter, 84
Bayer CropScience, 56
b-carotene, 86
  See also Golden rice
Beachy, Robert, 49–50
Beddington, John, 62
Bees, 17, 18, 34

D

E